TREE ADVENTURES IN YOSEMITE VALLEY

TREE ADVENTURES
IN
YOSEMITE VALLEY

by Rod Haulenbeek

Wide-(eye)d Publications
P. O. Box 964
Carnelian Bay, CA 96140

Library of Congress Catalog Card Number: 94-90129

ISBN: 1-885155-02-6

Printed and bound in the United States of America.

Printing Information   1 2 3 4 5 6 7 8 9 10

This book is dedicated to all those people who ever loved the trees of Yosemite Valley, and marvelled, and wondered...

HOW TO USE THIS BOOK

This book has four kinds of Tree Adventures in it. Adventures 1 through 3 are Adventures in Identification of 25 kinds of trees and 16 kinds of shrubs found in the Valley, through examples with exact locations. Adventures 4 and 5 are Adventures in Landscaping, exploring what man has done with trees in the Valley. Adventures 6 and 7 are Adventures in Magnificence of individual trees. Adventure 8 is an Adventure in Time and Color. There are also three Appendices.

Adventure 1 introduces you to the three main kinds of trees in the Valley, but it also gives some principles about these trees which will be useful in later adventures. Time required: 2 to 3 hours.

Adventure 2 takes you around the free Shuttle Bus route. All you do is get off the bus and follow this guide. You will learn all you need to know at this bus stop in the time it takes until the next bus comes. If you only have time for one Adventure, this one is the best: it will introduce the rest of the trees native to the Valley at one to three per bus stop. The stop descriptions are designed so that you can start anywhere along the route. This chapter also asks questions followed by a number in brackets. The answers are not obvious; my answers are in Appendix A in the back of the book. Time required: 4 to 6 hours.

Adventure 3 takes you on a tour of the garden in back of the Yosemite Museum. The garden has not only native and non-native trees but also some shrubs and wildflowers commonly seen in the Valley. This Adventure is for people who are curious about how gardens change over time, or who want a convenient way to see trees from other areas of the Park. Time required: 2 to 3 hours.

Adventure 4 is an exploration of the Ahwahnee Hotel area, with its extensive landscaping. This Adventure is for people who want to see a well-thought-out landscaped area. Time required: 2 to 3 hours.

Adventure 5 is a history and archeology Adventure, one which takes you to a place which was a thriving village 70 years ago but which is now only rocks and trees; this is the Old Village between Sentinel Bridge and the Chapel. This Adventure requires imagination and observation. Appendix B is for those who want more information. Time required: 3 to 4 hours.

Adventure 6 is for people who love to look at magnificent specimens of trees, whether they be the tallest, thickest or most grizzled. Instructions are given on how to find these trees, which are all within 100 feet of a road or trail. This Adventure also tells you where large stumps may be found. Time required: 4 to 6 hours.

Adventure 7 is for those people who love Giant Sequoias. There are 47 of them in the Valley, all planted by settlers; and if you would like to go on a Giant Sequoia hunt, this Adventure is for you. All the trees are along or near the Shuttle Bus route. Time required: 4 to 6 hours.

Adventure 8 is for people who want to know what to see any month of the year . Since you already know where different kinds of trees are, you can check out how they look whenever you visit. Time required: 1 year!

Appendix C gives the Latin names for all plants mentioned in this book, because common names are not always precise.

Many of the people who come to Yosemite Valley are repeat visitors; this book was designed so that they can take one or more Adventures this trip, and some more on the next trip. Also, the Adventures are almost independent, so you don't need to go in any particular order; although it will help you to go through the first five Adventures first. I have included Treasure Maps with some Adventures, because you will be seeking true Treasures.

FOREWORD

Imagine how Yosemite Valley would look with another type of vegetation. If it were in a rain forest setting you would rarely be able to see the muddy waterfalls because of the thick, choking mist, constant low clouds and swarming mosquitoes; you could only see the next tree. If it were in a desert setting you would see scrubby cactus and only occasional water cascading from the precipitous Valley walls. If it were in an alpine setting you would see sparsely scattered stunted trees covered with snow eight months a year, with no waterfalls because there was only ice.

Now look at the Valley as it is: with lush forests of trees with various green leaf colors, trunks of shades of red-brown to gray, through which you can see the picturesque streams and rivers, the cream to gray Valley Walls with their crystal, sparkling waterfalls against a deep blue sky studded with puffy white clouds. All this in what I like to call "the biggest flat spot in the Sierra", a unique place where trees grow huge rapidly.

For me, the forests made Yosemite Valley such a beautiful place that they inspired me to find out more about Sierra trees.

There are books about the geology, history, rock-climbing and points of interest about Yosemite Valley; and there are books about Sierra Nevada trees; but there are no books about the awe-inspiring trees of Yosemite Valley. So I decided to write about them.

As I see it, there are three types of visitors to the Valley. The first type drive around the Valley but never get out of their vehicles except to eat. The second type park and immediately lace up their hiking boots, fill their backpacks or check their climbing gear en route to an intimate look at Yosemite's wonders.

The third group arrives here disoriented and with never enough time to spend but with a burning desire to Contact Nature. If you are reading this, you are probably in this group, and this book was written for you.

I prepared this book featuring what I would like in a nature guidebook: a conversational tone; a series of Adventures (for they truly are) at a comfortable, non-strenuous walking pace on the flat Valley floor; illustrations which would help identify Nature's works of art without being art themselves; and large enough type so that the book could be read easily in the low light level of the woods.

Come join me as I go on eight Tree Adventures in Yosemite Valley!

THANKS TO...

Librarian Linda Eade and Park Historian Jim Snyder of the NPS for helping me search for relevant literature.

Bob Fry, Dean Shenk, Sean Eagan and Lisa Acree of the NPS for information about local botany and history.

Shirley Sargent and Moira Donohoe for their perspectives on local history.

Yosemite Transportation Services bus drivers, who have observed and read much about Valley trees, for numerous delightful conversations about the trees and for things to check out.

Stan Hutchinson for information about Valley Giant Sequoias.

George Murphy, Elita Flores, Dean Shenk, Shirley Sargent, Ron Hamman, Alan Bragg and Chris Hamma for "road-testing" Adventures and constructive comments about the manuscript.

Pat Watson for help with map generation.

The countless people who understood the value and relevance of this project and encouraged me to continue this project during times of discouragement and frustration.

TABLE OF CONTENTS

On the Cover: This is part of the bark of the Incense Cedar tree near Swinging Bridge (mentioned in Adventure 6). Galen Clark built his cabin under this tree, and sawed off the branches on one side up to about 80 feet to prevent large limbs from falling on his house.

ADVENTURE 1

The Three Main Tree Species of the Valley

Visitors to the Valley cannot help but notice three species of trees. There are pines which frequently reach three to five feet in diameter, are 150 to 200 feet tall (in almost every case the tallest trees around), and sometimes have bark that looks like an alligator's skin. There are also other evergreens which are as wide as the pines but not as tall, with full symmetrical foliage and with dark brown or cinnamon (sometimes ropelike) bark. Last, there are broadleaved trees which spread majestically in areas like Yosemite Village, with huge, gnarled or broken limbs.

These three trees are Ponderosa Pine, Incense Cedar and California Black Oak, and they make up perhaps 95 percent of all trees in Yosemite Valley; they are the subject of this Adventure.

This Adventure starts at Shuttle Bus Stop 10, in front of the Village Store. I'm including a Treasure Map to orient you. But first let's discuss some things about trees which may help you in all your other adventures in this book.

Ponderosa Pine

The sketch on the next page will help you identify Ponderosa Pine, which is not only dominant in this immediate area but is the most widespread conifer in the Western United States. Ponderosas make the other trees, large trees in their own right, seem puny by comparison. To me, a combination of characteristics of Ponderosa Pine and Yosemite Valley team up to make these trees dominant:

1) Ponderosa Pine is a conifer, and conifers are better adapted to this climate than broadleaved trees are. Needle-shaped conifer leaves have a small surface area compared to their volume, so they do not lose water as readily as broad leaves do during the long, dry

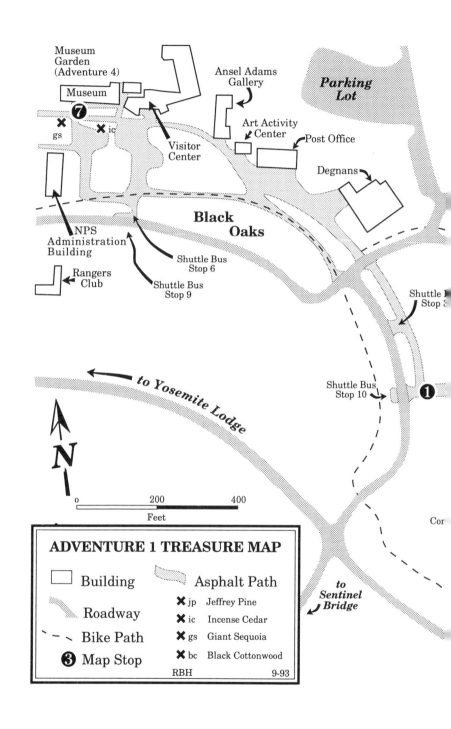

Museum
Garden
(Adventure 4)

Museum

❼

✖ gs   ✖ ic

Museum
Garden
(Adventure 4)

Ansel Adams
Gallery

*Parking
Lot*

Art Activity
↙ Center

Post Office

Visitor
Center

Degnans ↘

**Black
Oaks**

↙ NPS
Administration
Building

Shuttle Bus
Stop 6

Rangers ←
Club

Shuttle Bus
Stop 9

Shuttle I
Stop ?

Shuttle Bus
Stop 10 ↘

❶

← *to Yosemite Lodge*

N

0   200   400

Feet

Cor

*to
Sentinel
↙ Bridge*

ADVENTURE 1 TREASURE MAP

☐ Building   Asphalt Path

Roadway   ✖ jp   Jeffrey Pine

' - - Bike Path   ✖ ic   Incense Cedar

❸ Map Stop   ✖ gs   Giant Sequoia

                           ✖ bc   Black Cottonwood

RBH   9-93

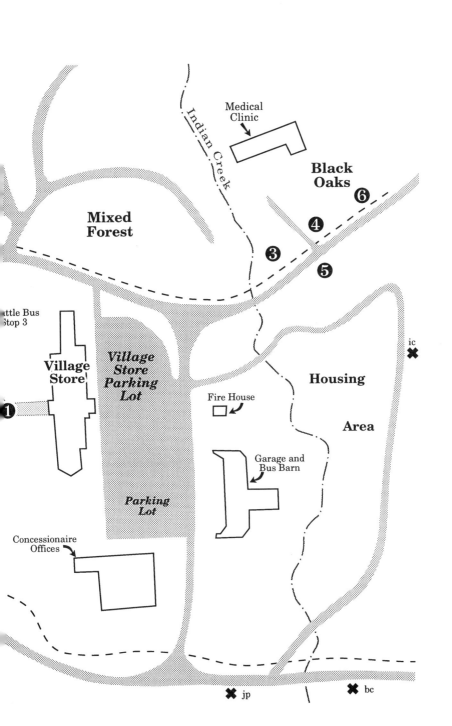

Indian Creek

Medical
Clinic

Black
Oaks

⑥

④

③

⑤

Mixed
Forest

ttle Bus
top 3

Village
Store

*Village
Store
Parking
Lot*

Housing

Area

Fire House

❶

*Parking
Lot*

Garage and
Bus Barn

Concessionaire
Offices

ic ✖

✖ jp

✖ bc

summers here. Needles also stay on conifer trees for more than one year, so the trees don't have to use energy to make leaves each year. And since leaves stay on the trees during the relatively mild Sierra winters at this elevation, the trees can photosynthesize (grow) all winter.

2) Conifers with single straight trunks can grow to great heights without breaking limbs: broadleaved trees usually branch into several main limbs, and these are more liable to break than a single trunk (if in doubt, ask a Mechanical Engineer about this one).

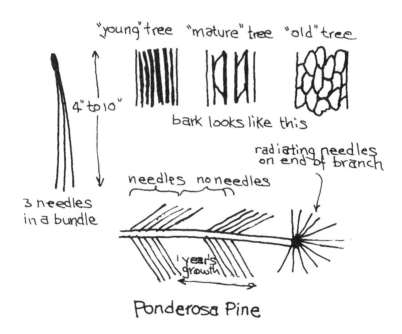

Ponderosa Pine

3) Pines such as Ponderosa have a long root in the middle called a "tap root", which in Ponderosa Pine seedlings grows even longer than the seedling's height in order for the tree to find a steady supply of underground water. If there is a dry year and the ground near the surface dries out, the trees can still satisfy their water requirements with the tap root.

4) Ponderosa Pine can grow in a wide range of conditions: any type of soil, on a slope facing any direction, near water or on a crack in a rock, in any area with annual precipitation of 10 to 50 inches. All it needs is a sunny location — in a shady location, the shade-intolerant Ponderosa would not prosper.

5) Ponderosa Pine grows as rapidly to great heights as any of the other species with which it grows; that 200-foot-tall tree you see in the Valley may be only 60 years old.

Speaking of size and age, how do you tell how old a Yosemite Valley Ponderosa is? There are three ways.

The first way is by looking at its bark. Look at some of the young trees around you; their bark is dark with deep, black, vertical furrows. As the tree grows older, the furrows become more indistinct as the lighter-colored high parts become wider; in an old tree the bark looks like alligator skin, and the bark breaks off in pieces about the size and shape of picture puzzle pieces. The twin-trunked Ponderosa between Shuttle Bus Stop 10 and the Village Store entrance (Stop 1 on the map) is a good example of a mature to old tree. Compare this tree's bark with that of the other trees around this area.

The second way is to count the horizontal branches. Each spring, a Ponderosa sends out four or so horizontal twigs, arranged radially, and a vertical twig. The next year the sightly taller tree does the same thing, and the distance between that year's twig and the one from the previous year is how much the tree grew vertically during that year. So you just have to count number of horizontal branches. This method is easier for young trees which have all their horizontal branches, and harder for older trees which have lost some lower branches. But no problem: usually you can see branch scars on the bark (incidentally, this method works well for most pines and firs, but does not work for Incense Cedars). Check out some of the Ponderosas in the area and see if the horizontal branches radiate like I say; then go to an Incense Cedar and notice that the branches seem to come out of the trunk at random.

Growth Charts

If you have counted branches on a few trees, you may have noticed that, after a tree becomes about 50 feet tall, it is hard to see the branches, let alone count them. So the third way may be better for older and taller trees. It uses the charts on the next page.

These charts show how fast and tall the three most common Valley trees — Ponderosa Pine, Incense Cedar and California Black Oak — grow in the Valley. The charts are from my informal survey of age versus diameter of stumps and diameter versus height of standing trees. Note that the Ponderosa grows more rapidly in both width and height than the other two trees.

The curves are only averages of a number of trees I measured. In fact, there is a great variation in size for all trees because local growing conditions play an important role in the tree's growth. For example, a Ponderosa in an "unfavorable location", such as under the shade of another tree or in a dry place away from a reliable water source, may grow to less than an inch in diameter in the first 10 years, while a nearby tree may grow to 6 inches in diameter; likewise, 100-year-old Ponderosas vary from 23 to 63 inches in diameter. To get my information on diameter versus age, I looked at many tree stumps. A "typical" Ponderosa stump is shown in the diagram below (the "seats" at Bus Stop 10 are actually slices of Ponderosa Pine, so you can look at them too).

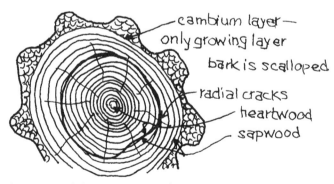

cambium layer —
only growing layer
bark is scalloped
radial cracks
heartwood
sapwood

rings tend to be concentric

Typical Ponderosa Pine Stump

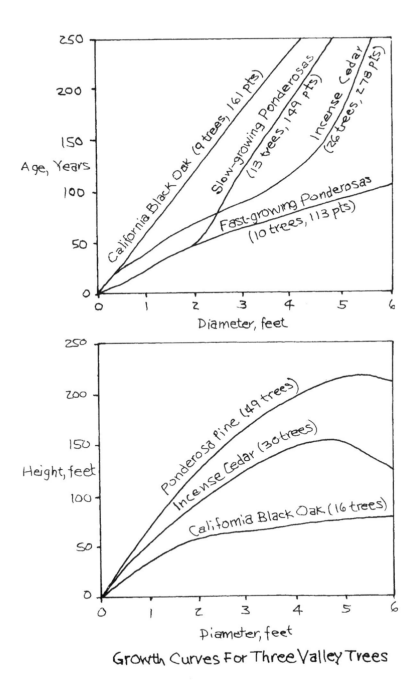

Growth Curves For Three Valley Trees

A tree trunk has different parts, each with its own functions; and a tree stump gives us an opportunity to look at them. To visualize what's going on, think of a tree trunk as similar to your arm. The three main parts of an arm are the skin, the flesh (the muscle) and the bone; these correspond to the bark, the sapwood and the heartwood of a tree trunk.

Bark works like our skin does for us; its main function is to protect the tissues inside it. If a person's arm skin is destroyed, bacteria can cause infections and the person may be in danger of dying. Likewise, if a large part of the tree's bark is destroyed, the tree will be in danger of dying. This is because right inside the bark is the "cambium layer", which is actually the only part of the tree where cells are splitting (where the tree is actually growing). If the bark is destroyed or removed all around the tree, the cambium layer is at the mercy of outside forces--including heat, cold and disease.

The microscopic cambium layer is only a few cells thick. When a cell in this layer divides, it sometimes makes one bark cell and one trunk cell; the rest of the time it makes two trunk cells. Trunk cells have thinner walls during springtime, when there is plenty of water available and it is not too hot; they have thicker walls when the weather is hot and dry or in the winter when the sun doesn't give off as much energy. The net result is that there are two rings per year. The later ring is usually darker in color and raised compared to the earlier ring; and with two distinct types of rings we can tell how old the tree is.

Note that the outer part of the stump is darker in color (especially in damp weather). This is called the "sapwood", and it is through this part of the tree that water comes up from the roots and nutrients to make the tree go throughout the tree. Although these cells are not "alive", they act as pipes for the fluids necessary for tree life. The inner part of the tree is generally lighter in color. This is called the "heartwood", and the reason it is lighter (especially in damp weather) is that no fluid can come through it. The tree has filled all the holes here with resin, which is like epoxy cement, and fluids can no longer pass through. The reason for this seems to be to give the tree strength; the heartwood has the same sort of functions as our bones do for us.

Let's check out some Ponderosa stumps. The edges of any of the roads and trails in the Valley are good places, though you may have to walk a little bit to find stumps. Between the entrance to Curry Village Cafeteria and the Curry Village Post Office there is a 2-foot-high Ponderosa stump. But there are also a few stumps near here. Let's go walking.

At the north edge of the Village Store parking lot is a large stump (Stop 2).

Go across the east-west road and walk along the asphalt path. On your left you will see not only Ponderosa Pines but also another kind of tree, Incense Cedar.

Incense Cedar

The sketch below will help you identify Incense Cedar. Cones of the Incense Cedar are only about an inch long and are shaped like a fleur-de-lis, with only three to five scales (unlike the Ponderosa cone with a hundred or more scales). To find a cone, look under a mature or old tree in Fall or Winter. You may find no cones or just a few cones instead of the hundreds you will find under Ponderosas.

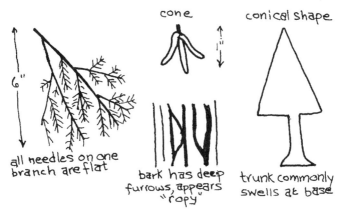

cone   conical shape

6"

all needles on one branch are flat

bark has deep furrows, appears "ropy"

trunk commonly swells at base

Incense Cedar

Many people mistake Incense Cedar for Giant Sequoia, because the bark looks similar and old trees have cinnamon-colored bark (as a matter of fact, even I have trouble distinguishing them

from a distance). However, your chance of finding a Giant
Sequoia tree in the Valley is about 1,000 to 1, and your chance of
finding an Incense Cedar is about 2 to 1. So if you see a tree you
think might be a Giant Sequoia, the odds are against you. (Later
in this Adventure and in Adventure 4 we will see Incense Cedar
and Giant Sequoia side by side and can compare them.)

In almost every case, Incense Cedars found with Ponderosa
Pines are more numerous but smaller in size. This is because they
don't grow as fast and because they don't grow as tall. However,
they can tolerate shade much better than the pines, and so don't
need to grow so tall so fast. The growth curves show the differences
between the two trees.

In a Ponderosa-Incense Cedar forest you will probably see
small Incense Cedars, because Incense Cedars are shade-tolerant;
but you will see very few small Ponderosa trees, because Ponderosa
seedlings rarely survive in the shady deep forest. Look into the
nearby forest for an example of this.

A typical Incense Cedar stump (see the sketch below) differs
from a typical Ponderosa stump in three ways: 1) generally the
rings are more closely spaced than those of a Ponderosa stump
(because Incense Cedar thickens more slowly); 2) the heartwood
is rotted out (because the Incense Cedar is more susceptible to
heartrot than the Ponderosa); 3) the rings near the bark tend to be
more wavy-shaped (because Incense Cedar trunks frequently
swell out near ground level).

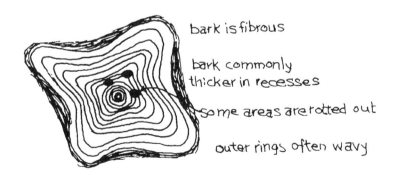

bark is fibrous

bark commonly
thicker in recesses

some areas are rotted out

outer rings often wavy

Typical Incense Cedar Stump

Why would these trees swell out near ground level? Consider this: in most trees in the Valley, the trunks are vertical, the roots are horizontal, and they are connected. So somewhere the tree has to make that right angle. In Ponderosa Pine this usually occurs below the surface (so the stump has round rings), but in Incense Cedars this usually occurs just above the surface (so the stump has wavy rings). Check out this concept on a few trees near you .

The best places to look at Incense Cedar stumps are the Cabin-without-bath area of Yosemite Lodge and the open area between Curry Village Cafeteria and Curry Village Registration Building.

Walk along the bike path to the east until you cross the bridge over the creek (Stop 3). There a number of stumps of both Ponderosa Pine and Incense Cedar in this area; see if you can tell the difference.

Walk further along the bike path until you are in front of the Medical Clinic (Stop 4). This area has fewer Ponderosa Pine and Incense Cedar trees, but it has some marvelous California Black Oak trees.

California Black Oak

The sketch below will help you identify California Black Oak, which makes up many of the mature trees in this area.

bark has 1" rectangles

bark gray to black

dead limbs on ground

acorns fall in September

leaves have pointed lobes

leaves turn yellow in October

4" to 8"

California Black Oak

This was an acorn orchard in one of the main Miwok Indian villages of the Valley. To prevent wildfires from destroying their orchards, the Miwoks burned the area around each tree when vegetation was small rather than big, and in the process burned up seedlings of Ponderosa and Incense Cedar. This also helped the oaks prosper, because Black Oak is even more intolerant of shade than Ponderosa Pine, and a tall Ponderosa or Incense Cedar shading an oak might either decrease the acorn crop or kill the oak.

The growth curves show that oaks grow more slowly and only grow a third to a half as tall as the other two trees; when the other trees get taller they may rob sunlight from the oaks.

California Black Oaks grow all over the Valley, but in conifer stands grow taller and skinnier, with much less spread, than in the Village area. In fact, you can tell where there were oak orchards by looking for trees with wide spreads. The sketch below is of a California Black Oak stump.

You can see either stumps of entire trees or stumps of limbs cut off near the trunk if you go to places where there are a lot of large spreading oaks. The rings are normally thinner than those of the other two trees, and the "wood rays" from the center of the stump to the edge are more prominent than the rings. This is how to identify an oak stump.

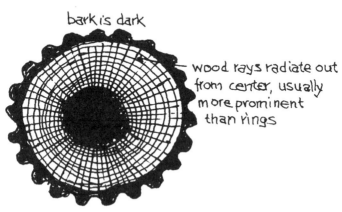

bark is dark

wood rays radiate out from center, usually more prominent than rings

heartwood is commonly rotted out

Typical California Black Oak Stump

There are two nice oak stumps near here. The first is across the street at Stop 5; it shows all the features of the diagram. The other great oak stump is along the bike path about 100 feet further at Stop 6); this stump still has all its sapwood, but its heartwood has been rotted out by a fungus which produces a phenomenon called "heartrot".

Heartrot is present in most of the old California Black Oak trees in the Valley, and is responsible for those fallen limbs you see near many California Black Oaks. The fungus only attacks the heartwood, but this provides the strength to hold up the limb, and when the heartwood is gone, the limb falls. Amazingly enough, though, a California Black Oak can have lost almost all its major limbs and still apparently thrive.

Another major pest of the California Black Oak is Dwarf Mistletoe. If you look up into the branches of almost any old oak, you will see the mistletoe. Dwarf Mistletoe does not usually kill the tree, but may weaken it so that it dies from other causes.

Head west on the bike path, and as you go admire the mixed Ponderosa Pine/Incense Cedar/California Black Oak woods between the Medical Clinic and Degnan's. At Degnan's, go on the asphalt to the right for a few hundred feet (admiring the beautiful oaks with their wide crowns and fallen limbs), passing the Post Office, Ansel Adams Gallery and Visitor Center, until you finally come to the front door of the Yosemite Museum (Stop 7).

From the front door of the Museum, you can see two trees only a few feet apart. The one slightly to the left about 50 feet ahead of you is an Incense Cedar. The one the same distance from the entrance and a little to the right is a Giant Sequoia. From the entrance the trees may look similar, but go up to the two trees. Not only is the foliage different, but the Incense Cedar bark is hard to the touch and the Giant Sequoia bark is springy to the touch. This may be your first sighting of a Giant Sequoia tree in the Valley, but there are 46 more of them (covered in Adventure 6).

In this adventure we have explored the three main large trees of the Valley, and to me they make the Valley more beautiful. They also complement each other. The gnarled, spreading oaks with their bright green foliage (or naked limbs in winter) contrast well with the conical, lush dark green Incense Cedars and the lofty Ponderosas. These in turn set off the majestic granite cliffs, the bright blue sky and the cascading waterfalls. I think that without any of these elements the Valley might not be so beautiful. What do you think?

ADVENTURE **2**

On the Shuttle Bus Route

In this Adventure, you will learn to identify 19 different kinds of trees and 5 different kinds of shrubs commonly growing in the Valley. But this will be easy, because the free Shuttle Bus system will provide your transportation (so you only have to wander around at the various stops between buses); and fun, because I'll show you only one to five kinds of plants at each stop (so you won't be overwhelmed). Also, if you are in doubt as to what kind of tree or shrub you are seeing as you go around the Valley, you can always go back to the bus stop where you first saw the plant and relearn your identification.

This Adventure doesn't need a Treasure Map, because there is one at each bus stop. And this Adventure is flexible — you can start at any bus stop, because the descriptions are almost totally independent of each other. I'm providing sketches of each kind of tree or shrub next to the description. These sketches are not intended to be Art, just to help you find the real Works of Art (the trees themselves). You may notice numbers in brackets in the text. Just for fun, I'm asking you some questions without easy answers, things to think about. I have my "answers" in Appendix A. So try your luck, if you feel like it, and see how your answers compare with mine.

Stop 1 (Same as Stop 14). Curry Village...Cultivated Trees

As you get off the bus, look into the parking lot. Among the cars are a number of trees with drooping branches. These are mostly apple trees, probably planted around 1880 by Yosemite pioneer James Lamon, who came here to homestead in the 1850s. Homesteaders had to prove residence or cultivation for five years, and planting orchards was a convenient way to do this. The trees, once started, required little maintenance, and the homesteader didn't have to even live on the land; he could get someone living in the valley to pick the fruits for him. There is evidence that there were a great number of such orchards in the Valley at one time. Only three orchards and a few trees here and there attest to this phase of the Valley's history; other orchards either could not survive where they were planted or were removed during further development.

Around 1925 the National Park Service (seeing a need for expansion parking in Curry Village) designated this area as a parking lot, and apparently removed every third row to make room for cars. Right now they are experimenting by spraying some trees with water to wash the blossoms away so no fruit is produced (because apples falling on your car might dent it; also because the bears who visit Curry Village like them a lot!).

Note the California Black Oaks between the bus stops and the parking lot; they are described at Stop 6. These are magnificent old trees, cared for by the Indians who lived in a village here, and who harvested acorns from the trees. At the forward end of Stop 14 there is a four-foot-diameter stump of a California Black Oak tree. Go to the stump and count rings, which are much closer together than the rings of most Incense Cedar and Ponderosa Pine trees in their stumps in the valley. The oaks were very slow-growing, reaching the heights of the old trees near the parking lot in perhaps two or three hundred years. This compares with the 150-to-200-foot heights of the Ponderosas, which were probably reached in less than 100 years.

Stop 2. Lower River Campground...Pacific Dogwood

Behind the bus stop, among the 200-foot Ponderosas and somewhat shorter Incense Cedars, there are some trees 20 to 30 feet high with bent, crooked trunks. These are Pacific Dogwood trees. If you are seeing them in either summer or winter, you are missing a treat, because they may be the most colorful trees in the Valley. During Spring they are loaded with six-petaled flowers (technically they are leaves, but why get technical?) up to 6 inches across, and during the fall the foliage turns pale reddish with clusters of bright red berries. This tree is similar to the Eastern Dogwood, but is not the same species. The Eastern Dogwood has only four petals, and the petals are much smaller. This brings up a mystery. Why are these two Dogwood species so different? Is it climatic conditions? [2.2]

The dogwoods are so much shorter than the Ponderosas that it seems they should be shaded out and not survive. However, a study has shown that Dogwoods thrive best in 1/3 of the light needed for ordinary trees. If you planted a dogwood in your front yard with no tall trees for shade (like I did once), it would likely die; dogwoods prefer shady, moist sites like this.

This is a good place to check out two more things. The first is the small wire mesh or plastic tubes across the road, which have

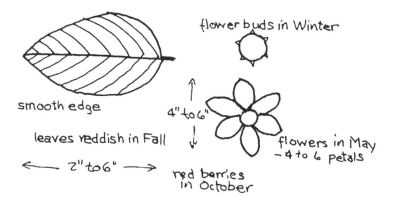

Pacific Dogwood

California Black Oak seedlings in them. It was noticed a number of years ago that there were very few young oak seedlings in the Valley; as a result, volunteers have been transplanting seedlings since 1985. These seedlings are particularly relished by the local mule deer population, so the tubes are there to protect the seedlings. Go to a few of these and see how the seedlings are doing. Do you think the tubes are large enough? I don't.

The second thing to check out is the dead pine trees down by the Merced River. Some of the trees were cut down near the ground, and their stumps are very interesting-looking. Some of the trees were cut down recently, and the wood doesn't look too rotted (check out the heartwood — it is reddish in newly-cut stumps and whitish in older stumps).

There are other trees with bleached or partly-rotted stumps; and still other stumps that seem to have some sap coming out of the heartwood. Some trees fell over without being cut down. Many of these fell with their tops downriver. This may be because the Mono Winds, which topple trees in the Valley, come from the East and are strongest along the river where there are fewer trees to break the wind force.

Stop 3. Village Store...River Plants

Walk toward the Village Store entrance. You will notice a huge Ponderosa tree with a split trunk. Either this is two trees which have grown together or one tree which has split. Which do you think it is? [2.3]

Between this tree and the store entrance, beneath the boardwalk, there are many trees and shrubs along the streambed. Although they were obviously planted here, all like to grow near running water.

The two main trees at this stop are White Alder and Quaking Aspen. White Alder has three identifying features. The first feature is the green pointed leaves with toothed edges. The second feature is an eye-shaped scar pattern with a round eyehole below and an eyebrow above where branches have fallen off the trunk. The third feature is the 3/4 inch "pine cones" among the leaves. Alder cones from another state, plated with metal, are sold as "pine cone" jewelry inside the store; but this tree is nothing like a pine. The "cones" give positive identification of the tree in Winter.

Quaking Aspen looks a lot like the White Alder except for a couple of features. First, the aspen leaves are roundish with toothed edges. Second, the White Alder trunk branches out just a few feet from the ground, while the Quaking Aspen generally does not branch until near the top of the tree. Third, the Quaking Aspen

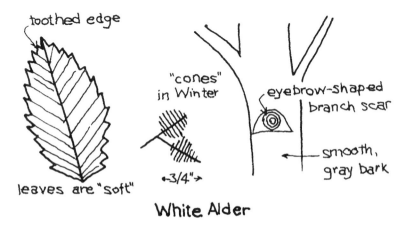

toothed edge

"cones" in Winter

←3/4"→

eyebrow-shaped branch scar

smooth, gray bark

leaves are "soft"

White Alder

trunk is a very light yellowish color instead of the gray of White Alder. Fourth and best, when the wind blows Quaking Aspen leaves twirl about because of the way they are attached to the twig.

Both types of tree were planted at the edge of the wooden deck south of the store entrance. See if you can tell which is which.

Since all these trees are short-lived, probably in 70 years none of the trees you see today will be here. In their place other trees of the same kind will spring up.

There are three main shrubs here. Creek Dogwood looks like Pacific Dogwood (described in Stop 2), but there are three differences. The first difference is that the Creek Dogwood doesn't have the huge "petals" of the Pacific Dogwood...but you could only distinguish these in May. The second difference is that this is a shrub rather than a tree (generally a shrub has many trunks of small diameter coming out of the ground rather than one larger trunk). The third difference is that the youngest Creek Dogwood twigs are maroon-colored.

The second shrub is Spice Bush (described at Stop 7 of Adventure 3), which has pointed leaves up to six inches long and beautiful brownish red flowers in June. The third shrub is Dwarf Maple, which looks a lot like Bigleaf Maple (described at Stop 5), but which has many small trunks.

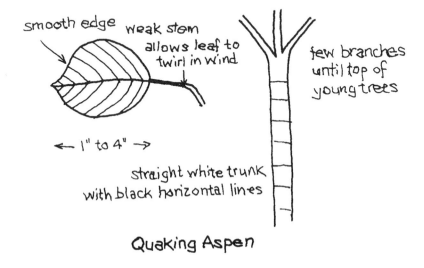

smooth edge   weak stem allows leaf to twirl in wind

few branches until top of young trees

← 1" to 4" →

straight white trunk with black horizontal lines

Quaking Aspen

Stop 4. Ahwahnee Hotel...Giant Sequoia

The Ahwahnee Hotel grounds have been landscaped with many interesting trees, some of which are described in Adventure 4. This description will only include the area near the Shuttle Bus stop.

As you get off the bus, look to the right of the hotel. There is a line of conifers in the parking lot with drooping branches and a nice conical shape. These are Giant Sequoias (Bigtrees). As you look at them, notice that they are not all the same size, even though they were all planted at the same time (probably around 1930). The one on your left, in particular, is smalller than all the others. Why do you suppose that the trees are different sizes? [2.4]

Walk over to the line of trees. Notice that, after the fifth tree, there are a couple of trees spaced more closely and not as tall. It's pretty obvious what happened here. One or two trees died and they were replaced with Incense Cedars. The landscapers might have thought that people would not notice that the Incense Cedars were similar-looking but actually different trees. But we're smarter than that, right? This brings up an interesting point about Sequoia and Incense Cedar trees—they look quite similar; in fact, many visitors to the Valley mistake Incense Cedars for Giant Sequoias.

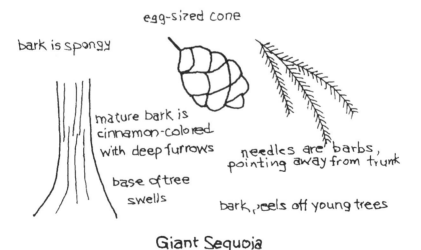

egg-sized cone

bark is spongy

mature bark is cinnamon-colored with deep furrows

needles are barbs, pointing away from trunk

base of tree swells

bark peels off young trees

Giant Sequoia

Look at the differences between the two trees. First, the Giant Sequoia has twigs that are rounded and long, with sharp barbs on the twig pointing outward from the tree; Incense Cedar has flat-looking twigs that seem to keep branching out. Second, high up in young Giant Sequoia trees such as these the leaves and branches seem to form round masses, while in Incense Cedars they form flattish masses. Third and best, walk up to a Giant Sequoia and gently press on the bark. Note that it is a little spongy (I call it soft). The Incense Cedar bark, on the other hand, is hard to the touch.

For me the Giant Sequoia is an amazing tree. From close up the twigs look flimsy and thin, yet from farther back the foliage looks full. Also, Giant Sequoias grow large extemely quickly—these trees are less than 70 years old at press time yet are up to five feet in diameter and 160 feet high. And they are almost like castles in being perfect defense mechanisms—they are almost impervious to fires, insects and fungus.

Around this particular parking lot there are four other Giant Sequoia trees. Now that you can recognize this kind of tree, see if you can find these four trees.

Stop 5. Degnan's Building...Bigleaf Maple

Along the west face of the Degnan Building next to the bus stop is a group of Bigleaf Maple trees. They are easily recognized by their big, three-lobed leaves. Go down the sidewalk 100 yards or so to the Village Store entrance, past the twin-trunked Ponderosa to the creek. There is a Dwarf Maple growing there; compare the trunks and leaves of the two trees.

Next to the south entry to the Degnans Building there is a Quaking Aspen tree about 30 feet high and eight inches wide. This is a fast-growing tree: Twenty years ago it was a sapling five feet high with an inch-wide trunk. Of course, Quaking Aspens are short-lived too; this tree will probably die before it reaches 60 years old. Look at the bark. Though young Quaking Aspen trees have horizontal lines, the older trees have blackish patterns. Since this tree's bark is so soft, people have carved their initials in it. This particular tree, with no other trees around it competing for light, spread out more than the Quaking Aspens near the deck of the Village Store, which were planted more closely together.

While you're waiting for the bus, check out the wooden seats. These are sections of Ponderosa Pine trees; the National Park Service calls them "rounds". These particular rounds are from

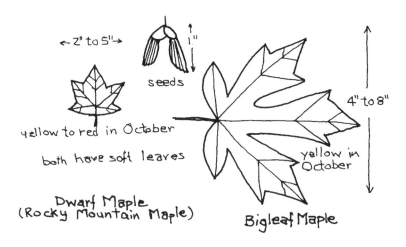

←2" to 5"→

seeds

1"

4" to 8"

yellow to red in October

both have soft leaves

yellow in October

Dwarf Maple
(Rocky Mountain Maple)

Bigleaf Maple

trees in the Valley which grew rapidly (see how far apart the rings are) and died at around 100 years old. Either they blew down during one of the frequent windstorms in the Valley or the Park Service cut them down after they died. The Park Service removes these "hazard trees" from places where dead trees might fall on people (that's why there are so many stumps at the edges of roads and paths).

It's hard to tell which part of the log the rounds came from, because Ponderosa trunks have almost the same thickness for 100 feet or more. Compare the rings from a few of the stumps. Sometimes the first few rings are close together (the tree is trying to establish itself); then the rings are wide for 20 to 50 years, and they thin again. Sometimes a ring isn't the same thickness all around the stump and sometimes the rings are much thinner for a few years. Why is this? [2.5]

Stop 6 (Same as Stop 9). Visitor Center...An Indian Orchard

Note the huge dead limbs of the California Black Oak trees around the bus stop. These limbs fell off the trees after the heartwood (which provides structural strength for the limbs) was destroyed by fungus. Look at a few limbs lying on the ground. Commonly, the outside part of the bark (the sapwood) is intact but the inside part of the trunk (the heartwood) is rotted away.

Some of the downed limbs may have Dwarf Mistletoe still attached. It's easy to recognize Dwarf Mistletoe — it has a lot of small branches radiating out from a point, and commonly the tree limb is swelled at that point; it also has small, flat, thick leaves. Dwarf Mistletoe shortcuts plant metabolic processes by tapping its roots right into the water- and sugar-conducting tissues of the oak tree, thereby getting a "free ride" and hurting the oak tree's chances of survival at the same time. Incidentally, dwarf mistletoe is found in conifer trees in the valley too, but it is a more serious problem in Black Oaks.

bark has 1" rectangles

bark gray to black

acorns fall in September

leaves have pointes   es

leaves turn yellow in October

dead limbs on ground

California Black Oak

Although you might think that the combination of massive decay and a parasite would kill the tree, look at the old trees; despite battle scars and fallen limbs, the live parts of the trees seem to be healthy.

You may notice some cylinders of either wire mesh or plastic a couple inches across. These contain California Black Oak seedlings and were planted by volunteers after a National Park Service survey showed that there were few young trees in the meadows of the Valley. The cylinders are to protect the young trees from deer, who relish the young leaves within their reach.

Notice the little rope fences. These were put up in certain areas of the Valley to protect the fragile plants from being trampled by the millions of tourists walking around in these areas annually.

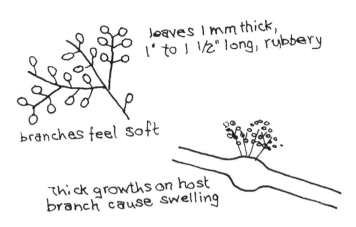

leaves 1 mm thick, 1" to 1 1/2" long, rubbery

branches feel soft

Thick growths on host branch cause swelling

Dwarf Mistletoe

Stop 7. Lower Yosemite Falls...Canyon Live Oak and California Laurel

If you are stopping here, I am assuming that you are going to the Falls, so this description is of the area near the base of this awesome waterfall.

As you take in the thunder of the waterfall and the beauty of the water falling down on the rocks, sit down on the wooden bench nearest the creek. This bench is made from part of a Ponderosa Pine tree. Note how far apart the rings are. This tree grew very quickly (16" diameter in just 10 years!). Now look at the outside of the log. It has lots of little holes in it. They don't look normal. What do you think caused those holes? [2.7]

There are many small trees and shrubs on the waterfall side of the paved area. Look first at the ones with the one-inch-long leaves. To me, these seem like trees that can't make up their minds: some of the leaves on each tree have smooth borders and some have sharp spines. This is one of the two main species of oak trees in the Valley, Canyon Live Oak. This tree is evergreen; it keeps at least some of its leaves all Winter, although you will see lots of dead leaves on the ground. Actually, the tree loses some of its leaves each year. This is incontrast to the California Black Oak seen at Stop 6, which loses all its leaves each year.

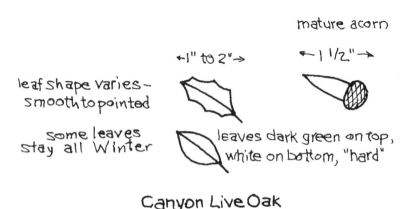

mature acorn

←1" to 2"→   ←1 1/2"→

leaf shape varies—
smooth to pointed

some leaves
stay all Winter

leaves dark green on top,
white on bottom, "hard"

Canyon Live Oak

Canyon Live Oak is frequently found on talus slopes, possibly because water percolates through the granite boulders on the slopes, giving this tree plenty of water. In contrast, California Black Oak seems to prefer the flat Valley bottom.

The waterfall above you is so big that it makes the 30-to-40-foot-high Canyon Live Oaks look like shrubs.

There is another common broadleaf tree near the path and paved area. This is the California Laurel, also called the California Bay because of the odor and taste of its leaves. Gently but firmly rub a leaf and then smell your fingers; the bay leaf is commonly used for seasoning food.

The tall cone-bearing trees are Douglas Firs. Note that the tallest trees do not have a symmetrical shape; instead the foliage seems very irregular. This is characteristic of Douglas Fir. The trees in this area are the largest and oldest seen anywhere on the Shuttle Bus route except those at Stop 16 (where this species is described).

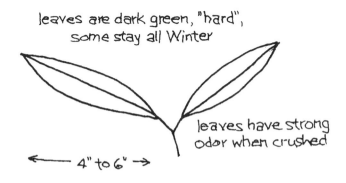

leaves are dark green, "hard", some stay all Winter

leaves have strong odor when crushed

← 4" to 6" →

California Bay (or Laurel)

Stop 8. Yosemite Lodge...Sugar Pine

Walk back from the bus about 100 yards. A Sugar Pine is visible from the Shuttle Bus route in a triangle of dirt between three asphalt paths in front of the Hemlock Building of Yosemite Lodge. This tree is a young one (maybe 30 to 40 years old), but it is deformed at the top and probably will never be a beautiful tree; it was obviously planted here. In former times there may have been many Sugar Pines in the the Valley, but if there were almost all are gone now in what may be the biggest riddle of the Valley — where did they go?

Look at the needles from a few feet away and you can tell that this tree somehow doesn't look like any of the Ponderosas surrounding it. Look more closely at the individual needles and you will see that there are five in a bundle. This tree, when mature, has a distinctive shape, not to mention the cones a foot or more long which dangle from branches 150 feet from the ground. You can see many fine Sugar Pines on Highway 41 between Wawona Tunnel and the turnoff to Glacier Point Fresno and on Highway 120 around the turnoff to Tioga Road.

Two large Ponderosa Pine trees with "puzzle bark" frame the Registration Building; these also make a great frame for a picture of Upper Yosemite Falls.

Sugar Pine

To the right of the benches there is an Incense Cedar stump. A the time of writing there is still bark clinging to the stump. This bark is characteristic of Incense Cedar bark.

Look at the tall, symmetrical conifer about 50 feet to the right of the Registration Building; it looks like a Christmas tree. In fact, this particular tree is decorated with colored lights at Christmastime. This tree is a White Fir, which is described more fully at Stop 12. Firs are popular Christmas trees. Why? Look at the tree from a distance and then go a little closer. [2.8]

Under this treee are some bushes about six feet high. These are Western Azaleas—native but landscaped in this location. They have beautiful flowers in Summer.

To the right of the sidewalk leading to the inner part of the Lodge area is a tree with large, five-lobed leaves. In late winter it is the first tree to leaf out; in late summer, before it loses its leaves, it has lush dark green foliage; in fall, large brown fruits contrast with its naked branches. This plant is the California Buckeye. It is not native to the Valley, but it is common in the drier foothills west of the Valley. The fruit of this tree stuns fish, so the Indians used it in fishing.

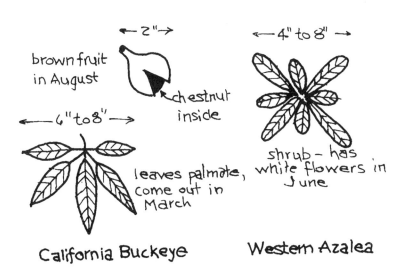

brown fruit in August — ← 2" → — chestnut inside

← 6" to 8" → — leaves palmate, come out in March

← 4" to 8" → — shrub - has white flowers in June

California Buckeye   Western Azalea

Stop 9 (Same as Stop 6)

Stop 10.   Village Store...Non-native Trees

As you get off the bus, walk ahead of the bus until you are across the road from the bank building. The beat-up looking pine tree that doesn't really look like a Ponderosa is a Lodgepole Pine. This tree can be distinguished from a Ponderosa because 1) The needles are one to two inches long instead of six; 2) There are two needles in a bundle instead of three; 3) The cones are much smaller. This particular tree also has round orange growths on some branches (possibly the tree's defense against insect attack).

Since Lodgepole Pine grows so slowly, and since it is so intolerant of shade, it only has a growth advantage when there is a disturbance to more tolerant trees such as other pines and firs. Lodgepole and Quaking Aspen are frequently the first trees to come back after a forest fire.

Lodgepoles have another adaptation to forest fire. In its native habitat the tree's cones may stay on the tree up to 20 years; in that time, if there is a forest fire, the tree dies but the heat melts the resin holding the seeds in the cone. The seeds then fall on the sterilized earth and germinate after the fire has passed. For this reason pure thick stands of Lodgepole seedlings are common in the High Country in burned areas. (Incidentally, Quaking Aspen are also common in burned areas because new saplings sprout from the ground where the old tree's root system went.)

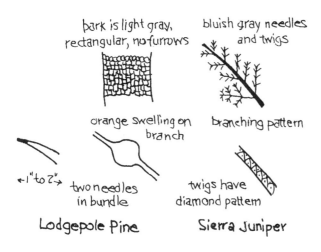

bark is light gray, rectangular, no furrows

bluish gray needles and twigs

orange swelling on branch

branching pattern

←1" to 2"→ two needles in bundle

twigs have diamond pattern

Lodgepole Pine   Sierra Juniper

Although Lodgepoles have the greatest elevation range of any forest tree in the U. S. (sea level to 11,000 feet), they don't thrive in the Valley; they grow best in Yosemite at elevations of 7500 to 10,000 feet. The few trees in the Valley probably grew from seeds carried from the High Country in floods and planted near the river.

On the path between the Village Store entrance and the Quaking Aspen grove is another tree not usually seen in the Valley, an evergreen which looks a little bit like Incense Cedar. This tree, a Sierra Juniper, is grayish green and has green twigs with white lines around them. It normally grows at the same elevation as the Lodgepole Pine; but unlike the Lodgepole, it has to be transplanted in the Valley.

Walk on the paved pathway (the "Pedestrian Mall"), towards Yosemite Falls. On the right of the path you will see a bush with gnarled reddish or purplish brown branches and with round leaves about the size of a 50-cent piece. This bush is Manzanita. Although it is found around the Valley, it is normally on exposed dry slopes (such as on the Upper Yosemite Falls Trail), because it is almost a desert-type plant. Its many small leaves collect lots of sun energy but have small surface area to protect the plant from too much water loss during the dry Sierra summers.

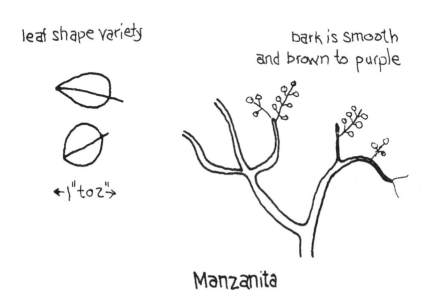

leaf shape variety

←1" to 2"→

bark is smooth
and brown to purple

Manzanita

Stop 11. Sentinel Bridge...Black Cottonwood

Cross the bridge on the left (east) walkway to the end of the stonework and look to your left at the three broadleaved trees alongside the river. Two of these are White Alders; the middle tree is a Black Cottonwood. The differences between the two trees are the light-gray bark and smooth glossy leaves of the cottonwood versus the gray bark and toothed leaves of the alder. The cottonwood is developing the mature bark shown in the sketch below.

Along the riverside path downstream from the bridge you will see some "old" cottonwoods perhaps 60 to 90 years old. (Although Black Cottonwoods grow very rapidly — up to one inch diameter per year — they start to deteriorate after 30 to 35 years.) These trees frequently have limbs and branches lying on the ground around them, broken off during snowstorms or windstorms because the wood is so brittle.

Black Cottonwood is in the same genus as Quaking Aspen (Stop 3); the main distinguishing features are the leaves, which are larger and more pointed in the cottonwood, and which shake in the slightest breeze in the aspen trees.

Look toward Yosemite Falls. The shrubs on the near-vertical walls are Canyon Live Oak trees (described in Stop 7) averaging 40 feet tall (which shows just how huge the waterfall is!). See the horizontal line of trees left of the falls? The roots of these trees get their needed water through large cracks in the rocks.

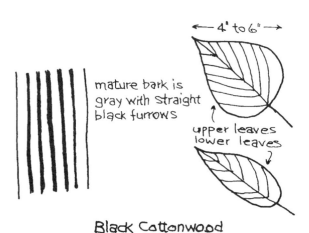

mature bark is gray with straight black furrows

← 4" to 6" →

upper leaves
lower leaves

Black Cottonwood

Although the oak trees are plentiful, there are few tall conifers on the side of the mountain. Why is this? [2.11]

Walk to the north edge of the parking lot and look at the large, spreading broadleaf tree on the other side of the meadow. This is an American Elm tree, planted by James Hutchings between 1864 and 1874. This tree, and the three Black Locust trees behind it, were planted along a road built when this area was fenced pasture. These trees are not native to the Valley, but may have been planted by Hutchings as a familiar tree in what must have seemed strange surroundings.

To me, this is the most beautiful tree in the Valley, with its gorgeous limbs spreading over open meadowland.

Look a little to your left on this edge of the meadow at the lone tree. This apple tree, planted in the 1880s, is one of the remnants of the old Village, which was mostly on the other side of the river and which extended from Sentinel Bridge to the Chapel. Adventure 5 will take you on a tour of the old townsite.

American Elm in Meadow
(View from other side)

Stop 12. Housekeeping Camp/LeConte Memorial...White Fir

As you get off the bus, look to the left and you will see a tall double Ponderosa Pine. Go over to it and look for branches between the two trunks. There aren't any, because there is not enough light in the middle. As conifer branches get shaded out, the tree kills these branches and they fall off.

Between the bus stop and the Ponderosa tree there is a mature White Fir tree. White Fir is easily distinguished from the other conifers in the Valley in four ways: first, its needles are either horizontal or curved slightly upward (unlike Douglas Fir, whose needles go out radially from the twigs); second, the needles from each branch are almost in a horizontal plane; third, young and mature trees have a "Christmas-tree" symmetrical shape (such as that seen at Stop 8); fourth, make a circle with your thumb and fingers around a twig and pull toward the end of the twig: Douglas Fir feels smooth and soft and White Fir feels hard and sharp. There are a number of young trees of each kind across the street. Go see if you can tell which is which.

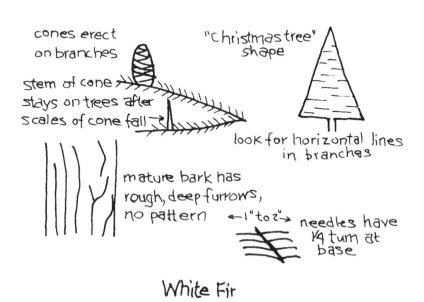

Left of the walkway to the LeConte Memorial there are three White Fir trees. Uphill from these three is a White Fir stump where the fourth tree was (compare the bark on the stump with that of the three live trees). Count the rings, and go to the age-versus-thickness chart in Adventure 1. Based on these trees, White Firs grow more slowly than Ponderosas.

White Firs can thrive under much taller trees because they are the most tolerant of shade of all trees in the Ponderosa Pine Zone.

In front of the LeConte Memorial there are two large shrubs. These are Blue Elderberry, and this is the only place along the Shuttle Bus route I spotted them. Nevertheless, they are very common in the Valley.

Blue Elderberry has compound leaves, and each leaflet has many small teeth along its edges. It is often used to make jams, jellies and pies, and is also used in the making of elderberry wine.

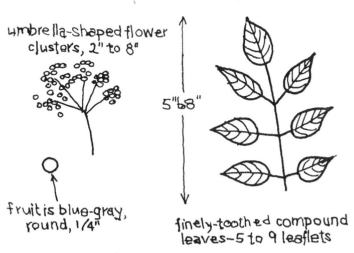

umbrella-shaped flower clusters, 2" to 8"

5" to 8"

fruit is blue-gray, round, 1/4"

finely-toothed compound leaves—5 to 9 leaflets

Blue Elderberry

Stop 13. Ice Rink...Black Locust

The bus doesn't stop here during the summer, but you can get here by getting off the bus at Stop 1/14 and walking along the road in the direction of Yosemite Falls. Go to the second driveway for the Curry Village Registration Building; just before it you will see a group of five trees resembling oaks from a distance but with strange-looking bark and foliage. These are Black Locust, a non-native species.

Individual leaves of Black Locust are round and about an inch in diameter. The leaf is compound, with several sets of small leaves opposite each other and one leaf on the end of the big leaf.

I think these trees were planted near Stoneman House, a luxury hotel built by the state when Yosemite was a state park. From its completion in 1888 until it burned down in 1896, the hotel was plagued with structural problems. A need was recognized for an upscale hotel in the Valley, however, and this need resulted in the building of the Ahwahnee in the 1920s.

An area of trees was cleared in front of this hotel, probably to enhance the view of the Valley walls. In this century, automobile campers drove onto the meadow in the lack of any rules protecting the vegetation; and sightseers watching the nightly "Firefall" until 1968 trampled the meadow.

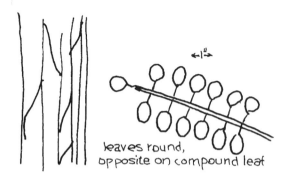

leaves round,
opposite on compound leaf

Black Locust

Stop 14 (Same as Stop 1)

Stop 15. Upper Pines Campground...The Forest Floor

Ponderosa Pines dominate this area. Look on the ground under them and you will notice a thick layer of brown pine needles (such stuff on the forest floor is called "duff"). Why are there so many dead needles lying on the ground when the trees look so healthy? Aren't these trees supposed to be evergreens?

They are: an evergreen is a tree which stay green because it doesn't lose all of the green leaves at one time. These trees shed their needles all the time (although more in Fall) but stay green because the average needle stays on the tree three years. Look at some of the trees near you; in the next year, about one third of the needles you see will have fallen onto the forest floor, to be replaced by new green needles.

There are also lots of cones on the forest floor. The tree sheds all its mature cones each year, and assuming that it takes a couple of years for the cones to decay, there are more cones on the ground than on the tree. Many of these cones are intact, but some have been chewed up by wildlife looking for seeds. In some cases, squirrels remove all the scales from the cone and leave little piles of scales on the forest floor; see if you can find some.

In a forest fire which only burns things at or near ground level, these needles and cones will be burned up, returning nutrients to the soil; sterilizing the ground so that seedlings have a head start over insects and fungi; and removing underbrush so the seedlings can get light. Obviously, Ponderosa seeds don't have a chance to get started in this area, so that's why you see no young Ponderosa trees. There are young Incense Cedar trees because these trees don't need to germinate on bare ground and can tolerate low light conditions in thick forest.

Stop 16. Happy Isles...Douglas Fir

This is the best bus stop for looking at Douglas Firs. There is a young one growing between two young Ponderosas on the left end of the bus stop as you get off. Look at the branches on these trees. The upper branches point upward, but the ones nearest the ground droop. This is quite normal for conifer trees. Check this out for yourself by looking at Ponderosa Pine, Incense Cedar, White Fir and Douglas Fir trees right around the bus stop.

To me, the drooping lower branches of young Douglas Fir are very graceful and beautiful; other people seem to agree — Douglas Fir is a very popular Christmas tree in this country: in 1964, 22 percent of American Christmas trees were Douglas Firs.

Douglas Fir has confused scientists for a century and a half since it was first encountered. Its similar appearance to firs was described at Stop 12; it has also been referred to as a Spruce, a Hemlock and "Oregon Pine". Botanists now classify it as a False Hemlock. In all, it has had 21 different common names. However it is classified, it is the most important timber tree of this country. Where it grows best, it is the tallest of all trees except the Coast Redwood.

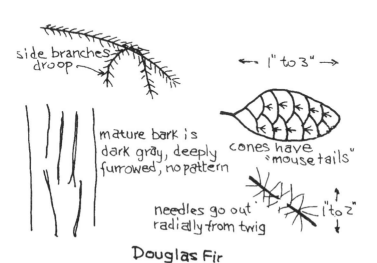

side branches droop

← 1" to 3" →

mature bark is dark gray, deeply furrowed, no pattern

cones have "mouse tails"

needles go out radially from twig

1" to 2"

Douglas Fir

Douglas Firs grow all over the Valley, but they grow best in moist, cool, shady areas like this one. They grow well near Yosemite Falls, on the south wall of the Valley where there is little or no sun in the winter, and at Mirror Lake. This is probably because they are more tolerant of shade than their main competitors, the Valley-dominating Ponderosas.

Stop 17. Mirror Lake...Willows

I'm assuming that if you stop here you are taking the 20 or 30 minute walk to Mirror Lake.

One of the earliest Pioneer trails in the Valley was made in the 1850s to Mirror Lake, probably following animal and Indian trails. This was possibly because this was a scenic spot, with its view of Half Dome, Mt. Watkins, Glacier Point, North Dome and of course the lake, which was much larger 140 years ago.

To enjoy this scenery best, go to the downstream end of the lake's north side. The rapids there somehow don't look quite normal. They are actually the remains of a series of dams built starting in 1882 to overcome the shrinking of this very important tourist attraction; the lake was filling with sediment from the High Country and Technological Man was trying to fight it. Altogether, four dams were built (one at the upstream end!), the lake was dredged, and finally Technological Man decided that this was not "natural". For the last number of years, the lake has been allowed to continue the process of change to a meadow like the meadows elsewhere in the Valley.

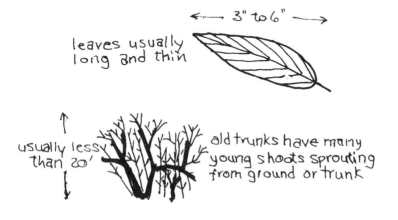

←— 3" to 6" —→

leaves usually long and thin

usually less than 20'

old trunks have many young shoots sprouting from ground or trunk

Willows

The lake is not only scenic but also a good place to compare the trees growing along watercourses. By now you should be able to recognize White Alders and Black Cottonwoods. But there is a third common tree here we haven't seen up close, the willow.

The willow genus has more than 14 species of similar-looking plants in the Sierra, so I'm going to lump them into one group. There are three main differences between willows and White Alders and Black Cottonwoods: willows generally have long, skinny, smooth leaves; they are more like many-trunked shrubs than trees (there are many branches seemingly sprouting out of gnarled trunks or the ground); and Sierra willows are almost always less than 30 feet tall, even in old age.

As you walk back down to the bus stop, look at the house-sized rock in the creek, and then look at the Valley cliffs. How did this rock get here? It seems to be too far from the cliff to have rolled from it. [2.17]

Stop 18. Stables...Vista and Sugar Pine Again

Look toward the stables as you get off the bus. You will see a few fruit trees such as those at Stop 1. This is one of the two orchards planted around 1860 by James Lamon, who claimed this land. Walk around the corral, down the path toward the kennel and up to one of the apple trees. Note that each one has a metal tag with a number. These trees have been catalogued by a consultant as part of the process of Valley vegetation restoration.

From the bus stop there is a nice view of the Glacier Point area and the south Valley Rim. If you have binoculars, use them to check out the trees on the rim. The four main types of trees areJeffrey Pine, White Fir, Red Fir and Sugar Pine (all these are described in Adventure 3). Because the climate is so much different there (with six months of deep snow cover, colder temperatures and frequent strong winds), White Fir is the only tree naturally occurring in the Valley Floor that can thrive on the Valley Rim. The vegetation zone of the Valley Rim is referred to as the Lodgepole Pine-Red Fir Belt.

The hill across the road seems strange in a valley with little elevation change. It is long and almost straight, and the Shuttle Bus route cuts through it between Stops 16 and 17. In a valley with little elevation change, this hill is unusual. The origin of this hill is debatable. Some authorities believe that it was deposited where two glaciers met (called a "medial moraine" by geologists). Others believe that it was deposited by rocks falling off Half Dome and going out onto the flat Valley Floor.

Wander up the hill to an Incense Cedar tree about 3 feet in diameter with a three-foot boulder resting on it. How did that boulder get there? [2.18]

At Clark's Bridge, where the Shuttle Bus route crosses the Merced River, there is a young Sugar Pine tree about a hundred feet tall. You can tell it is not a Ponderosa because its upper trunk is whitish and the clusters of needles is orange-size instead of basketball-size like Ponderosa leaf clusters. Note that there are two small Ponderosa trees growing up through the Sugar Pine's branches. From this you can tell the difference in the appearances of needle clusters. Look across the river a couple hundred yards upstream and you will see some more Sugar Pines, now that you know what to look for.

Sugar Pine is a major lumber tree because it has a tall, straight and thick trunk and has wood that "works" well. In theory, it should be common on the Valley Floor, because it frequently occurs with Ponderosa Pine in the Sierra. In reality, there are few Sugar Pine trees in the Valley, and only three young ones along the Shuttle Bus route (here and near Stops 8 and 17). Besides the trees upstream from here, there is one gigantic one next to Sugar Pine Bridge, and a few near Pohono Bridge on the western edge of the Yosemite Valley. This certainly is not many in a ten-square-mile area.

So why are there so few on the Valley floor? I have heard a number of explanations for this: they were all blown down in a windstorm in 1867; they were cut down for building materials in the Valley; the Valley elevation is too low for them to prosper.

None of these explanations satisfies me: the windstorm apparently blew down Ponderosa Pine and California Black Oak trees; before the turn of the Century only about 100 wooden buildings were built in the Valley (and at one mature tree per house that would not be enough to defoliate the Sugar Pines); and I've seen many Sugar Pines down to 3000 feet elevation.

I think it's because Sugar Pines are not aggressive trees like Ponderosas, and that they tend not to take over an area. If there were Sugar Pines in the Valley and the large trees were destroyed by fire, logging, insects or disease, it would be very difficult for the Sugar Pines to recover.

I've probably missed a few Sugar Pines, but all that I've seen that were not obviously landscaped were along the Merced River. This leads me to believe that the Valley Sugar Pines sprouted from seeds carried down from the High Country by the Merced River and its tributaries.

Stop 19. Lower Pines Campground...Another Vista

This is another good stop for looking at the Valley Walls and the trees on them. If you have binoculars, look through them at the Valley Rim. There are basically three types of trees there: Jeffrey Pine, Red Fir and Sugar Pine.

Look at North Dome. There is a group of 150-foot-high Jeffrey Pines and Red Firs near the bottom of the dome. This gives you an idea of the immensity of the Valley Wall: from the bottom of the trees to the top of the dome is 1000 feet, and the top of North Dome is 4000 feet above you.

Now look at Half Dome; you deserve a treat after all this work. Half Dome is Yosemite's most famous landmark. Its vertical cliff was carved by a combination of glaciation and a vertical zone of weak rock; its steeply-sloping sides and back were a result of erosion and exfoliation of the granite rock. The top of Half Dome is almost a mile above you. Some people see a face in the dark stains on the cliff — the face of Tissiack, in Ahwahneechee legend.

I can't think of a better way to end Adventure 2, which features a whole catalog of Yosemite Valley trees planted both by Man and Nature.

ADVENTURE 3

The Museum Garden

In this Adventure, we explore the area in back of the Yosemite Museum. Although today it is most visited for the model Ahwahneechee Indian village in its rear, the area was designed originally as a wildflower garden.

This garden had not only many kinds of wildflowers, both native and non-native to the Valley, but also had a number of trees and shrubs transplanted from other vegetation zones of the Park (most were from the Lodgepole Pine-Red Fir Belt). Many of these trees and shrubs are still living, and this Adventure is a quick and easy way for you to get to know these non-natives.

The Adventure starts at the back door of the Visitor Center in Yosemite Village. I'm including a Treasure Map to help you locate the features of the garden. I'm also giving you at least one use for each plant.

History of the Museum Garden

In 1931, an heiress to the Montgomery Ward fortune gave the Park a sum of money to spend in whatever way the Park Service deemed best. There had been some discussion about putting in a native plant garden in back of the Museum, and here were the necessary funds. That year the garden was started on a sand flat below Indian Canyon, in the sunniest part of the Valley.

Ranger-naturalist Enid Michael was chosen to supervise the planning and construction of the garden, as well as collection of plant species from both the Valley and other areas of the Park (mainly from higher elevations). She spent her summers in the Valley, helping the garden to evolve, until 1942.

The garden brook, added to keep the streamside plants happy, was artificial: water was pumped in at the top of the brook (in the back of the garden) and was removed at the bottom. At first, fast-growing trees were added to the trees already in the garden to help higher-altitude plants survive Valley summers; in 1936 some trees from higher altitudes were planted. By the late 1930s, the garden had about 600 species of native plants in 14 different simulated habitats from Valley level to tree-line level, and was receiving about 1000 visitors on the average summer day.

By the 1940s, there were only about 200 species surviving; today there are even fewer (partly because of lack of attention and partly because plants which grow robustly in this climate overcame weaker plants from other climates). However, a tour around this garden is the easiest way for Valley visitors to see good examples of trees and shrubs from other areas of the Park.

The Museum Garden Today

The map and accompanying stop descriptions are an attempt to give you a guided tour of the garden as it is today. This partial list of the trees, shrubs and wildflowers concentrates on the plants along the paths. Unless otherwise denoted, all these plants are Valley natives. Use the Treasure Map at the end of this Adventure to orient yourself; start at the back door of the Visitor Center.

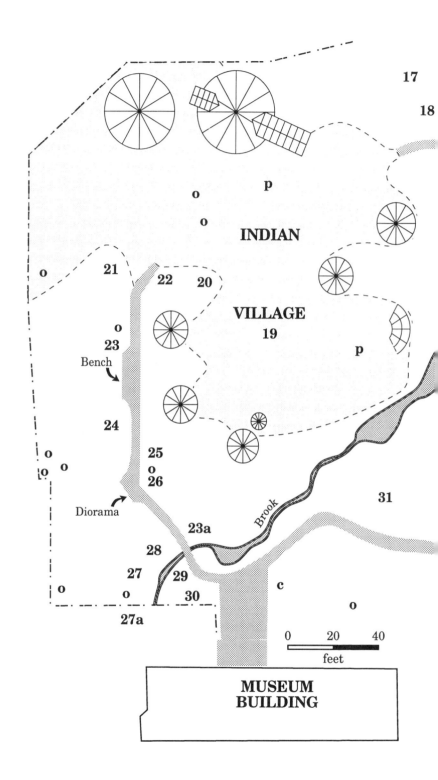

17

18

o

p

o

INDIAN

o

21   22   20

VILLAGE

o   19

23   p

Bench

24

25
o
26

Diorama   Brook

23a

28

27   29

30   c

27a   o

0   20   40

feet

**MUSEUM
BUILDING**

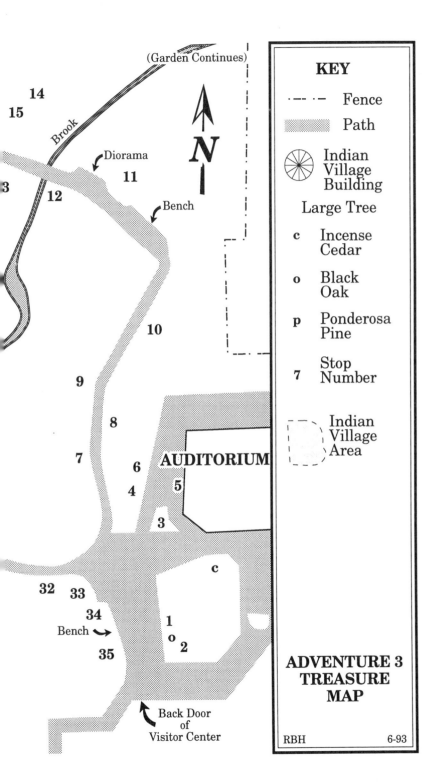

(Garden Continues)

14
15

Brook

3

Diorama

11

12

Bench

10

9

8

7

6

4

3

AUDITORIUM

5

c

32 33

34

Bench

35

1

o 2

Back Door
of
Visitor Center

KEY

—··—··— Fence

░░░░░ Path

⊛ Indian
Village
Building

Large Tree

c Incense
Cedar

o Black
Oak

p Ponderosa
Pine

7 Stop
Number

⌐ ¬ Indian
Village
Area

**ADVENTURE 3
TREASURE
MAP**

RBH   6-93

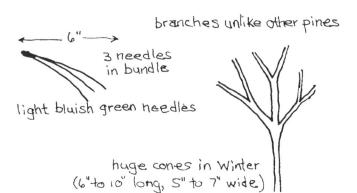

branches unlike other pines

←——— 6" ———→

3 needles
in bundle

light bluish green needles

huge cones in winter
(6" to 10" long, 5" to 7" wide)

Gray Pine

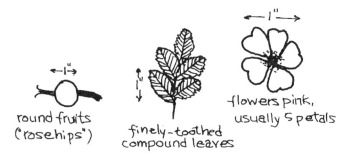

←—1"—→

round fruits
("rosehips")

←—1"—→

flowers pink,
usually 5 petals

finely-toothed
compound leaves

California Wild Rose

blooms in the evening all summer —
blooms die next day

4' to 6'

4" to 6"

6:53 PM   6:58 PM

Evening Primrose

Stop 1. Gray Pine (formerly called Digger Pine), is the taller pine (on the right, under the oak tree), with gray-green needles. It is one of five kinds of pines in the garden. Gray Pine has three needles in a bundle like the Ponderosa next to it, but of the pines in the Park only Gray Pine commonly branches at the top. Although Gray Pine is usually found in the foothills, it is quite common in Hetch Hetchy Valley, which at 3700 feet is only 300 feet lower than Yosemite Valley. Gray Pine seeds are sometimes strung together and sold as necklaces.

Stop 2. California Wild Rose is one of several wild rose species in the Sierra, all of which look quite similar; it is a Valley native. This shrub normally grows where the ground is frequently damp. The flowers are small but numerous and fragrant. The small, hard fruits, called "rose hips", are food for birds and some small mammals. Look for California Wild Rose in landscaped areas like the Yosemite Lodge Registration Building area.

Stop 3. Evening Primrose opens from a bud in five minutes or less each late spring and summer evening, as the amount of light decreases; the next day, the new flower shrivels in the sun. In the late 1930s an average of over 100 persons attended twice-a-week programs featuring the Evening Primrose flower buds opening in this garden. If you come in the late afternoon, you can see this phenomenon too. Try it! This plant is relished by deer. There are a few Evening Primroses around the Visitor Center.

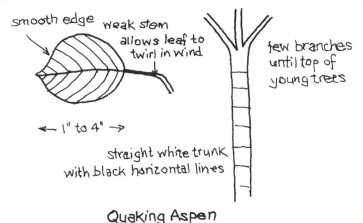

Quaking Aspen

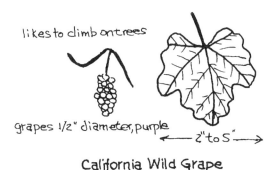

California Wild Grape

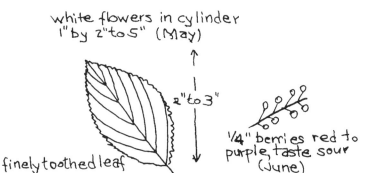

Chokecherry

Stop 4. These Quaking Aspens normally grow from the elevation of the Valley Rim to 10,000 feet (tree line), and can be identified by their white or yellowish bark and the wide pointed leaves which flutter in the slightest breeze. Quaking Aspen has the greatest areal distribution of any forest tree in North America. Since its wood is light and soft, it is used for paper pulp and excelsior; it works well, so it is also used for woodenware. Some Quaking Aspen trees are growing in Ahwahnee Meadow.

Stop 5. The California Wild Grape vine here does not produce grapes, but you can see that it is a fast-growing shrub (it was planted after 1970). The only vine which produces grapes near here is on the south side of the NPS Administration Building. Between the stone house and the Ahwahnee Hotel (Adventure 4) several trees are covered with these vines; in due time the vines may kill those trees by blocking out sunlight. The grapes have large seeds but are edible. Indians used grapevine like a natural rope to lash the beams of their buildings together.

Stop 6. Chokecherry is a Valley native shrub often used in landscaping in the Valley because of its showy white flower clusters. It is called "Chokecherry" because its plum-like fruits are too tart for most people to eat (though birds eat the fruits), but it can be used for jams and jellies. The Indians cooked chokecherry biscuits for children with stomach aches, and made a beautiful red dye with the juice. The leaves are bright yellow or orange in the Fall.

leaf shape variety

bark is smooth
and brown to purple

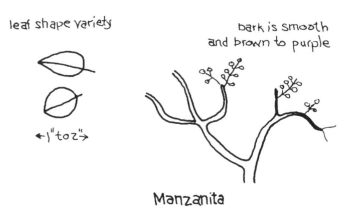

←1"to2"→

Manzanita

profuse white flowers on end
of twig (June and July)

foliage not very
dense

leaves soft
and opposite

four petals

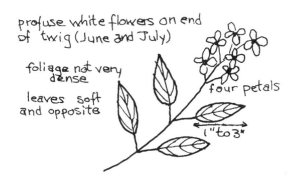

1"to 3"

Mock Orange

red-brown flowers (June)

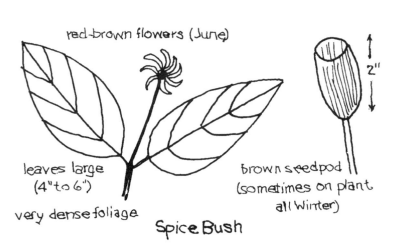

2"

leaves large
(4" to 6")

brown seedpod
(sometimes on plant
all Winter)

very dense foliage

Spice Bush

Stop 7. The shrub with the flat, thick leaves and gnarled, red-brown trunk is a Manzanita. It thrives on dry slopes (such as those on the Upper Yosemite Falls Trail). The wood is used for small wooden bric-a-bracs. Indians made cider from the berries, which are also eaten by wildlife such as birds, bears and chipmunks.

Stop 8. Mock Orange is another ornamental shrub. In June it has many small white flowers, and has attractive small leaves which are pleasing to the eye in the growing season. Some Indians made large Mock Orange branches into bows and small branches into arrow shafts. Look for Mock Orange in landscaped areas such as the Yosemite Lodge complex.

Stop 9. Spice Bush has pointed green leaves up to six inches long and three inches wide. Because it has a July-blooming beautiful red-brown flower with a pleasant aroma, it is very frequently used in landscaping around the Valley. It normally grows in the foothills, but there are a lot of these shrubs near Arch Rock on the western edge of the Park. Indians often used straight twigs for arrow shafts.

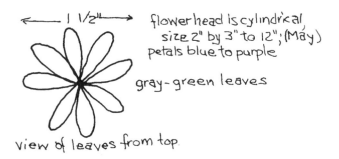

← 1 1/2" →

flower head is cylindrical,
   size 2" by 3" to 12"; (May)
petals blue to purple

gray-green leaves

view of leaves from top.

Bush Lupine

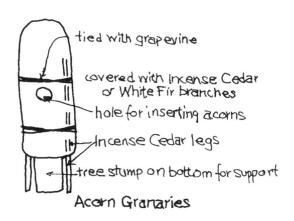

tied with grapevine

covered with Incense Cedar
   or White Fir branches

hole for inserting acorns

Incense Cedar legs

tree stump on bottom for support

Acorn Granaries

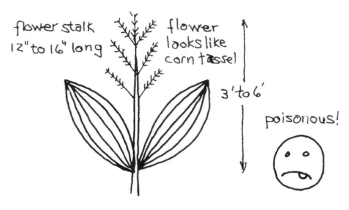

flower stalk
12" to 16" long

flower
looks like
corn tassel

3' to 6'

poisonous!

Corn Lily

Stop 10. Bush Lupine has showy blue or red-purple blooms in early summer, but its silvery foliage is showy during all of the growing season. There are a number of species of Lupines in the Park, all related to the Colorado Lupines and the Texas Bluebonnet. This particular species commonly grows up to 5 feet high. These plants are common along the roadside in areas of forest fires like the one on Highway 120 toward Crane Flat.

Stop 11. These curious-looking stands are acorn granaries such as used by the local Indians. The poles are of Incense Cedar, which can stand the weather for years without rotting. The covering for the granary is either White Fir, as in this case, or Incense Cedar. In these granaries, California Black Oak acorns dried out after being harvested in September and October, and supplied food all the next year.

Stop 12. Corn Lilies generally grow in wet situations (such as here next to the brook). Corn Lilies are highly poisonous plants, and were used by some Indians for birth control, and, in greater doses, for suicide. These plants are also poisonous to animals, who seem to leave them alone. Corn Lilies are easily spotted in the meadows around Crane Flat in the Spring.

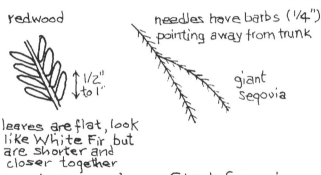

redwood

needles have barbs (1/4")
pointing away from trunk

giant
sequoia

↕ 1/2"
to 1"

leaves are flat, look
like White Fir, but
are shorter and
closer together

Coast Redwood vs. Giant Sequoia

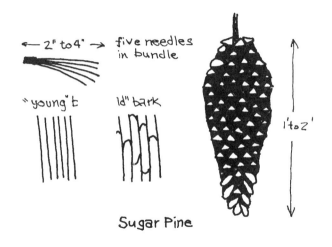

← 2" to 4" →   five needles
in bundle

"young" t   "old" bark

1' to 2'

Sugar Pine

bluish gray needles
and twigs

ws

branching pattern

twigs have
diamond pattern

Sierra Juniper

Stop 13. This tree is a Coast Redwood, native only to foggy areas along the coast of California. This tree was apparently planted here to contrast it with the Giant Sequoia tree at Stop 17. The third "Redwood", Dawn Redwood (native only to China), was also apparently planted in the garden but did not survive. Coast Redwoods are used as shingles, fence posts and grape stakes because the wood splits easily and does not rot, and these days for outdoor lawn furniture and decking. Coast Redwood is a common yard tree in the Central Valley of California.

Stop 14. About 40 feet from the path is a young Sugar Pine tree, planted as a small seedling in 1936. Except for two trees — the monarch at Sugar Pine Bridge near the Ahwahnee and one at Pohono Bridge — this is the nicest Sugar Pine I have seen in the Valley. Sugar Pines may have been used in the Valley to make siding and roofs for buildings. Indians used Sugar Pine pitch to coat places where arrowheads were lashed to shafts. There are some excellent stands of Sugar Pines along the highway near Crane Flat.

Stop 15. The small conifer to the left of the Sugar Pine and closer to the path is a Sierra Juniper. This tree was also planted in 1936, and looks fairly small for a tree that old. There are a lot of them across Tioga road from Tenaya Lake. These gnarled veterans rarely grow more than 60 feet tall, but they may be the oldest trees in the Park besides the Giant Sequoias, living perhaps several thousand years. Juniper saplings were used by some Indians for making bows; the berries were used by the Indians for treating rheumatism and for birth control. Today Juniper berries are used for flavoring gin, and the fruit are eaten by some birds.

egg-sized cone

bark is spongy

mature bark is cinnamon-colored with deep furrows

needles are barbs, pointing away from trunk

base of tree swells

bark peels off young trees

Giant Sequoia

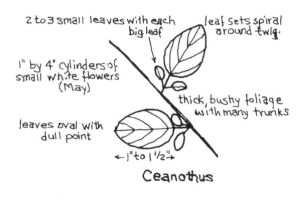

2 to 3 small leaves with each big leaf

leaf sets spiral around twig.

1" by 4" cylinders of small white flowers (May)

thick, bushy foliage with many trunks

leaves oval with dull point

←1" to 1½"→

Ceanothus

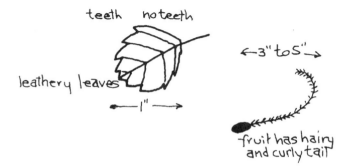

teeth   no teeth

←3" to 5"→

leathery leaves

←— 1" —→

fruit has hairy and curly tail

Birchleaf Mountain Mahogany

Stop 16. The tall tree to the left of the Sugar Pine tree is one of two young Giant Sequoia trees in this garden, also planted in 1936. Although this tree is almost as old as the one in front of the museum, it is not as large, probably because the site was not favorable. However, it is bigger than the one a few feet to the left of it planted at the same time in an even less favorable site.

Stop 17. In front of the taller conifers there is a Ceanothus shrub; this species is commonly called "Deerbrush". In the spring and early summer this plant has beautiful clusters of white flowers, which brighten the journeys on the highways going south and north out of the Park. This species of Ceanothus is often found in the forest, where it offers browse to deer, nesting sites to birds, and seeds to small rodents. Deerbrush is also sometimes used to make a tonic.

Stop 18. Birchleaf Mountain Mahogany is typically found in the Foothill Zone on the Western slope of the Sierra, where it sprouts readily after a fire. Note how "tough" the plant looks; it is known for its ability to resist cutting, fire, drought and heavy browsing by deer and other animals. Although the leaf looks like a birch leaf (hence the name), this plant is more closely related to the California Wild Rose at Stop 2. Like the rose, the wood was used by some Indians for dye-making. The wood is hard and its texture makes it useful for bric-a-bracs.

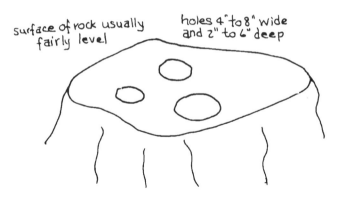

surface of rock usually fairly level

holes 4" to 8" wide and 2" to 6" deep

Grinding Rock

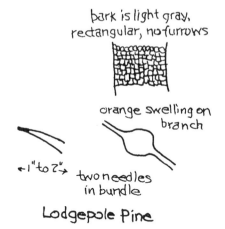

bark is light gray, rectangular, no furrows

orange swelling on branch

← 1" to 2" →   two needles in bundle

Lodgepole Pine

Feature	Ponderosa	Jeffrey
bark odor	no odor	smells like vanilla
cone size	generally smaller	generally larger
cone weight	lighter	heavier

Ponderosa Pine vs. Jeffrey Pine

Stop 19. In the center of the Indian Village there is a granitic rock with holes in its top. This rock was used by the local Indians to grind the acorns from California Black Oak trees into meal, in a step of preparation for a type of porridge.

Stop 20. This Lodgepole Pine tree was also planted in 1936, yet it is quite short compared to the Ponderosas and Sugar Pine. This species (which has two needles per bundle) grows better at the altitude of the Valley rim and above, but it still is a slow-growing tree. The presence of a grove of Lodgepole Pines of the same size is usually good evidence of a forest fire. Lodgepoles need a lot of light, and this shady spot may not be a favorable site for this tree. Lodgepole Pine is the most common tree along Tioga Road.

Stop 21. This tree and the one at the other side of the path look almost exactly the same to me. Now smell the bark of each one. The one on the left, with no smell, is one of the Valley-dominating Ponderosas; the one on the right, which smells like vanilla, is a Jeffrey Pine. There are a few Jeffrey Pines in the Valley; ttheir seeds were probably carried down from the High Country by river waters. Jeffrey Pine has two other distinctions. First, it is the host for an insect larva which was considered a delicacy by Paiute Indians; second, it is a source of heptane, a chemical used to calibrate octane ratings of gasoline. Jeffrey Pines are very common near Glacier Point.

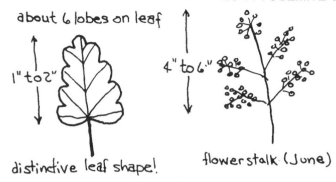

about 6 lobes on leaf

1" to 2"

4" to 6"

distinctive leaf shape!

flower stalk (June)

Creamberry

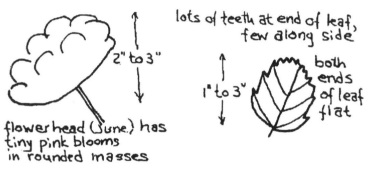

2" to 3"

flower head (June) has
tiny pink blooms
in rounded masses

lots of teeth at end of leaf,
few along side

1" to 3"

both
ends
of leaf
flat

Mountain Spirea

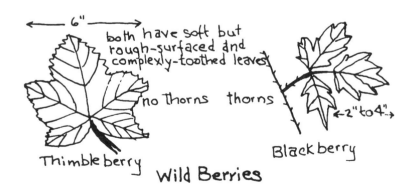

6"

both have soft but
rough-surfaced and
complexly-toothed leaves

no thorns   thorns

2" to 4"

Thimbleberry

Blackberry

Wild Berries

Stop 22. Under the Ponderosa Pine is a Creamberry bush, a plant which usually grows at altitudes from the Valley Rim to tree line at 10,000 feet on cliffs and rock ledges. I scoured quite a few books on uses of native Sierran plants but was unable to find any uses for this shrub; but I think that the flower spike and foliage are beautiful enough to qualify this bush as an ornamental.

Stop 23. This small plant is a Mountain Spirea, a relative of the Bridalwreath bush valued by gardeners, with its clusters of beautiful pinkish flowers. There are a number of larger ones at Stop 23A. It normally grows on the Valley Walls and Rim. Check out the tooth pattern on the leaves; there are lots of teeth on the end of the leaf but few on the sides. This is not only diagnostic of this species but extremely interesting. Mountain Spirea is an ornamental shrub, and I saw quite a few of them along the trail to Chilnualnua Falls near Wawona.

Stop 24. This area has wild blackberries (the plant with thorns and a three-lobed leaf) and thimbleberries (the plant with large flat three-lobed leaves and 3/4 inch 5-petaled flowers). Feel how soft the leaves are. Both these plants have edible berries which are often eaten by birds, can be eaten right off the bush, and are great for jellies, jams and preserves. They can be found in swampy areas.

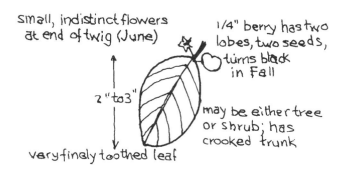

small, indistinct flowers at end of twig (June)

1/4" berry has two lobes, two seeds, turns black in Fall

2" to 3"

may be either tree or shrub; has crooked trunk

very finely toothed leaf

Sierra Coffeeberry

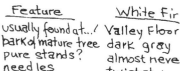

Feature	White Fir	Red Fir
usually found at...	Valley Floor	Valley Rim
bark of mature tree	dark gray	dark red
pure stands?	almost never	frequently
needles	twist at base, go away from twig	no twist at base, go along twig

Red Fir vs. White Fir

top of tree generally droops

needles radiate in groups, sometimes are blue-green

bottom branches droop to ground level

John Muir loved these trees!

Mountain Hemlock

Stop 25. This plant is a Sierra Coffeeberry. The American Forestry Association defines a tree as a plant growing to 12 feet or more, with one trunk larger than 9 1/2 inches in circumference (essentially 3 inches in diameter) at 4 1/2 feet above the ground; a shrub is shorter with multiple trunks coming out of the ground. How would you classify this plant? Sierra Coffeeberry is a large shrub with bark used by the Indians as a laxative.

Stop 26. This is perhaps the only Red Fir tree you will see in the Valley; its normal home is at the altitude of the Valley Rim. To distinguish between this and the White Firs over your left shoulder on the other side of the path, go to them and look at the place where the leaves meet the twig. There is a light yellow area where the leaf seems to be twisted one quarter turn. Now go back to the Red Fir and look in the same place. You will see that the leaves are not twisted at all. Also, the White Fir leaves go away from the twig immediately, while the Red Fir leaves go down the twig away from the trunk for a few millimeters. The Red Fir and Lodgepole Pine are the characteristic species of the next higher climatic zone than that of the Valley, and almost all of the trees near Badger Pass Ski Area are Red Firs.

Stop 27. Set back about 30 feet from the path, in front of the California Black Oak tree, is a grayish-green short conifer, a Mountain Hemlock. John Muir loved Mountain Hemlock because of its graceful, shape and drooping top. There is a nice stand of these trees along Tioga Road (between Tenaya Lake and Tuolumne Meadows), but this tree is not very impressive (it is probably a tree planted to honor someone in 1970). Just on the other side of the fence put up after the garden was established there is a larger tree, probably planted in 1936 (you can reach it easily by walking to the spot marked "27A" on the map).

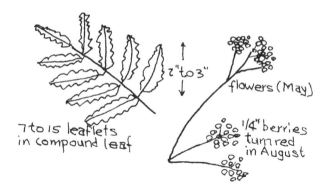

7 to 15 leaflets
in compound leaf

2" to 3"

flowers (May)

1/4" berries
turn red
in August

Mountain Ash

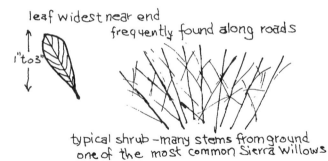

leaf widest near end

frequently found along roads

1" to 3"

typical shrub – many stems from ground
one of the most common Sierra Willows

Scouler Willow

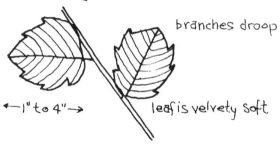

leaves have larger and smaller teeth

branches droop

←1" to 4"→

leaf is velvety soft

California Hazelnut

Stop 28. The shrub here with finely toothed compound leaves is a Mountain Ash. Most of the growing season it looks pretty unimpressive, but in late summer or early autumn it has showy clusters of red-orange berries, which are made into jams and jellies. Mountain Ash is normally found at the elevation of the Valley Rim. This tree, as well as trees at Stops 26 and 27, was planted here as part of a High Country plant association. I haven't seen Mountain Ash anywhere else in the Park.

Stop 29. Scouler Willow is one of the few easily distinguished willows, because its leaf is widest near the outer end. This shrub is one of the few willows which can grow away from water. Like Birchleaf Mountain Mahogany (Stop 18) it invades soon after forest fires. In October, the bright yellow leaves brighten the sides of Tioga Road, though this species is also native to the Valley. Some wood has a diamond-shaped pattern, making it useful for bric-a-bracs.

Stop 30. To the left of the maple is a California Hazlenut, which has a velvety soft (but not smooth) leaf — feel one. It produces a one-inch-long nut in a hairy sheath; the nut resembles a filbert. The bark was used by the Indians for making baskets and sieves. There is a large thicket of California Hazelnut on the front lawn of the Ahwahnee (see Adventure 4).

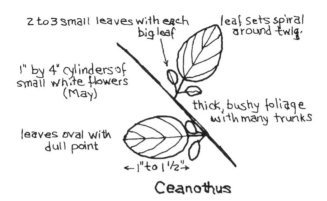

2 to 3 small leaves with each big leaf

leaf sets spiral around twig.

1" by 4" cylinders of small white flowers (May)

thick, bushy foliage with many trunks

leaves oval with dull point

←1" to 1 ½"→

Ceanothus

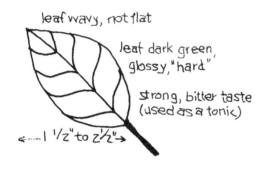

leaf wavy, not flat

leaf dark green, glossy, "hard"

strong, bitter taste (used as a tonic)

←····1 ½" to 2½"→

Quinine Bush

←2"→

brown fruit in August

chestnut inside

←6" to 8"→

leaves palmate, come out in March

California Buckeye

Stop 31. This is the same species of Ceanothus as at Stop 18, but in the spring this particular plant has blooms with a wonderful light lilac color.

Stop 32. This plant is called "Quinine Bush", because its leaves have a very sharp taste. It is a chaparral plant (native to the Foothills). Its leaves are leathery and have a curious wavy pattern. Another common name for this plant is "Bear Brush", probably because the early settlers thought bears liked this plant.

Stop 33. California Buckeye has a leaf with five lobes; this leaf shape is called "palmate" because it is shaped like a hand. Buckeye is also native to the Foothills. It is the first tree to lose its leaves (in late summer). Buckeye is a type of horse chestnut, and the nuts and twigs contain a neurotoxin which stuns fish. The Indians ground up the nuts and twigs to catch fish in this manner.

3" to 4"

acorn has woolly cap

underside of leaf is red-brown and woolly

1"

halfway between an oak and a chestnut

Tanbark Oak

1/8" bell-shaped pink blossoms (June)

1/2" white berries

1" to 2"

Snowberry

Stop 34. Tanbark Oak, a shrub intermediate between but neither an oak nor a chestnut, is native but rare here; it is common in the Coast Ranges of Washington and Oregon. As you might guess from the name, the bark of this bush contains much tannin and was used in the last century for tanning heavy hides.

Stop 35. Snowberry is the last plant in this guide. Like Canyon Live Oak and Black Cottonwood, its leaves vary in shape. The Miwoks used this Foothills native as a remedy for colds and stomach aches, and other Indians made arrows for small birds from the shoots. Today it is often planted as an ornamental plant because of its striking-looking fruits. Look for Snowberry in cool, damp, shady places.

Adventure 3 was a short tour through Yosemite Valley history and a good look at kinds of trees you may not see elsewhere on your Yosemite visit.

ADVENTURE 4

The Ahwahnee

In this Adventure we will explore the area around the Ahwahnee Hotel, built in the 1920s as a luxury hotel and landscaped over a period of four years. A Treasure Map is included to help you navigate.

The Adventure starts at Shuttle Bus Stop 3. Get off the bus and walk toward the covered porch. At the covered porch, take the path around the pond to your right (counterclockwise). This pond, like the creek in the Museum Garden (Adventure 3), is manmade; all the trees and shrubs were planted here, and together they have a very pleasing aspect. Let's look at the non-native trees around this pond.

Midway around the east side of the pond is a grove of Quaking Aspens (described at Shuttle Bus Stop 3 in Adventure 2) and Pacific Dogwoods. Both kinds of trees are quite showy in October: the pinkish leaves of the dogwood blend with the yellow leaves and thin white trunks of the aspens. A few feet past the footbridge on the north side of the pond is a Mountain Hemlock (described at Stop 27 in Adventure 3), the largest one in the Valley but still just a "baby". Where the path dead ends, look a few feet to the right at the Giant Sequoia (described at Stop 15 of Adventure 3), one of 25 planted on the Ahwahnee grounds; then go to the left down the west side of the pond. A few feet further, on your left, is a Sierra Juniper (described at Stop 16 in Adventure 3), also the largest in the Valley but also a "baby".

When you reach the porch again, walk under the porch and to the right along the sidewalk toward the parking lot, looking to the left over the fence; in the loading area of the hotel (Stop 1) are the two largest Black Locust trees in the Valley (see Shuttle Bus Stop 13 of Adventure 2).

As you look toward Yosemite Falls, you can see a line of 11 Giant Sequoias to your right in the middle of the parking lot; they are described at Stop 4 of Adventure 2.

Where the path ends, walk straight toward the northwest corner of the hotel building. Take the path between the Giant Sequoia and the corner of the hotel building; take the fork to the edge of the building and look at the two California Redbuds flanking the big picture window of the dining room (Stop 2). The sketch below shows how to identify these trees.

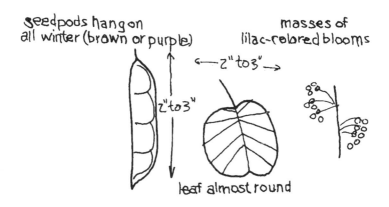

seedpods hang on
all winter (brown or purple)

masses of
lilac-colored blooms

←—2" to 3"—→

2" to 3"

leaf almost round

California Redbud

Go back to the fork and head down the path to the right, for that is the way of Tree Adventure. At the next fork 100 feet further look at the two pine trees a few feet to the right of the path at Stop 3. They look a little different from the Ponderosas; they are Knobcone Pines.

Knobcone Pine is native to the Valley but rare; I have only seen one other tree, in the National Park Service residential area. My guess is that that tree was probably planted between 1915 and 1920; it is on the Treasure Map for Adventure 7, and is listed in Adventure 6. The sketch on the next page shows some of the features of Knobcone Pine.

As you continue, look toward the tennis court at the spires of seven Giant Sequoia trees planted outside its north fence.

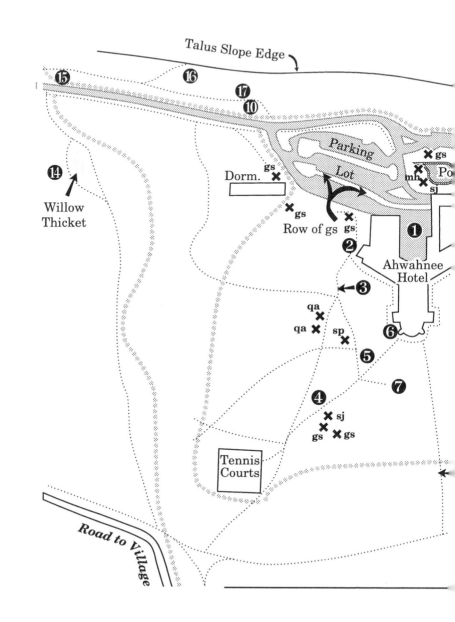

Talus Slope Edge

⑮

⑯

⑰
⑩

Parking

⑭

Willow
Thicket

Lot

gs

Dorm. ✗

Po

✗ gs

✗
mh

sj

✗ gs
Row of gs

✗ gs

❶

❷

Ahwahnee
Hotel

❸

qa
✗

qa ✗

sp
✗

❻

❺

❼

❹

✗ sj
✗
gs ✗ gs

Tennis
Courts

Road to Village

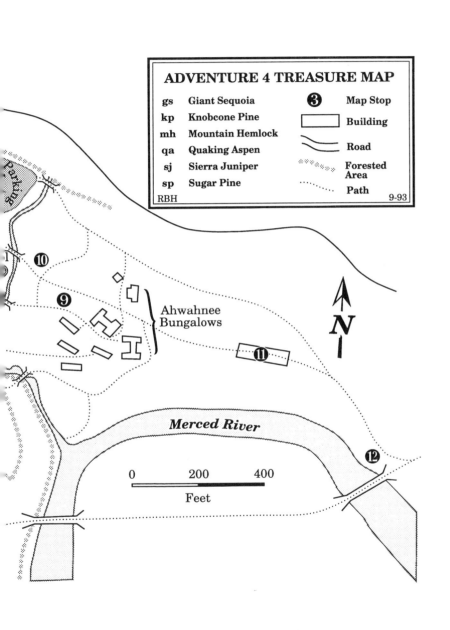

ADVENTURE 4 TREASURE MAP

gs	Giant Sequoia	❸	Map Stop
kp	Knobcone Pine	▭	Building
mh	Mountain Hemlock	〰	Road
qa	Quaking Aspen	⁘⁘⁘	Forested Area
sj	Sierra Juniper	⋯	Path
sp	Sugar Pine		

RBH   9-93

Parking

⑩

⑨

Ahwahnee
Bungalows

⑪

N

Merced River

⑫

0   200   400

Feet

←—3" to 5' —→

twig may grow around
the crooked cone

3 needles in bundle

grayer than Ponderosa

3" to 6"

Knobcone Pine

About 100 feet down the path is a crossing path. Continue on this path until you come to the second crossroads; turn left there. About 240 feet down this path, at Stop 4, you will see a grove of trees just to the right of the path. Among these are a multiple-trunked Sierra Juniper and two more Giant Sequoias. At the end of this grove is the best-developed thicket of California Hazelnut I have seen in the Valley. California Hazelnut is described at Stop 30 of Adventure 3.

About 50 feet farther you will come to a path intersection. Walk toward the hotel; about 60 feet past it you will see a Ponderosa Pine stump (Stop 5). This tree was cut down around 1990 and the stump is magnificent, so check it out.

Keep on this path until you reach the hotel. Next to the building, at Stop 6, is a California Bay tree. While it may not be the biggest in the Valley, it is a dandy, so I have listed it in Adventure 6.

Go back to the last intersection and turn to the left (south), walking on the lawn area as the path disappears. A one-to-two-foot raised area to the right of the path looks like a sand trap (Stop 7). That's probably what it was, because the front lawn of the Ahwahnee was a three-hole pitch-and-putt golf course until the 1970s! The lawn was the fairway. As a sometime golfer, I look at this as a rough course to play, with all the large oak trees all over the course. Look for other sand traps in the lawn area.

Although there is really no path in this lawn area, head toward the Giant Sequoia tree alongside the creek (Stop 8). This tree is easily the largest Giant Sequoia in the Valley. The exact planting date is undocumented, but my guess is the late 1880s. Note that the lower branches droop almost to the ground. This is typical of "young" Giant Sequoias. In their third century of life, these trees start to drop off the lowest branches; so in a couple hundred years the lowest branch of this tree might be 80 to 125 feet above ground level.

Walk up the flagstone path toward the right (east) of the hotel, noticing the Chokecherries (Stop 4 of Adventure 3) and California Bays (Stop 7 of Adventure 3), until you reach the footbridge across Royal Arch Creek. Cross the bridge and head east on the left asphalt path. In this area (Stop 9) there are many landscaped Rocky Mountain Maples (described at Stops 3 and 5 of Adventure 2). These turn yellow, orange and red in October, and are some of the most colorful trees in the Valley in Fall (along with the Pacific Dogwoods growing among them).

Back toward the footbridge, take the dirt path to the right (north). This path leads to one of the wonderful trees listed in Adventure 6, an aged Ponderosa Pine at Stop 10. This tree is 220 feet tall and 6.0 feet in diameter at 4 1/2 feet (the third largest Ponderosa Pine I have seen in the Valley); from the looks of its bark, it is a very old tree.

The path leading to this tree forks in front of the tree. About 100 feet down the right fork is a dirt road. Turn right on this road for about 600 feet, and stop where another dirt road joins it. To your right is a large concrete pad, about 170 feet by 50 feet (Stop 11). This was probably a recreation area for a campground here, called "Camp 8". This campground, which probably dates from the 1880s, was abandoned with the building of the Ahwahnee in 1926.

Keep going down the road until you see a stone bridge over the Merced River. This bridge is called "Sugar Pine Bridge" because of the huge tree between you and the riverbank (Stop 12). This aged Sugar Pine is the second widest tree I have seen in the Valley, at 185 feet tall and 8.1 feet diameter at 4 1/2 feet (the widest tree is an Incense Cedar 9 feet in diameter near El Capitan Bridge).

The boulders on the riverbank next to this tree were placed starting in 1886 to prevent the river from washing away the tree, a Valley tourist attraction in the late 19th century. This method of "controlling" erosion was used until almost three miles of these boulders had been placed on the Merced's banks in the Valley. But because it failed to control erosion and because there was a desire for more "natural" riverbanks, the Park Service is now removing stonework and replacing it with willow and Black Cottonwood trees, which they hope will accomplish the same task. (Go to the area around Housekeeping Bridge if you want to see both of these methods in use today)

Walk across the bridge to the right (west) on the asphalt path; about 800 feet later you will cross another bridge, Ahwahnee Bridge. Continue on until you can see the front of the Ahwahnee Hotel through the woods. Near a large metal plate there is a dirt footpath leading to the Ahwahnee; go down this path about 180 feet until you are almost at the hotel lawn area. On the left side of the path you will see a California Black Oak log (Stop 13). If you count the rings you will get an idea of the age of the graceful oak trees on the lawn.

Head back to the asphalt path and continue west until the path turns right at the roadway. Follow the bike path until you reach the meadow ahead of you and go along the dirt path toward the north Valley wall. This path is more or less the route of a paved road removed in the 1970s. As you walk, look a couple hundred feet to the left at the small grove of trees with a larger tree in the middle. These trees are Quaking Aspens, and the big tree is the largest tree of this species in the Valley (it is listed in Adventure 6). About two-thirds of the way across the meadow, at Stop 14, are two lone trewes and a thicket of grayish-green-leafed shrubs. The leaf shapes of these two kinds of trees show how much variation there is in willows.

As you cross the asphalt road at the north end of the meadow, look to the right at the stone house (Stop 15). In the early years of the Ahwahnee Hotel this was a gatehouse. Walk into the gatehouse and check out the roof, built somewhat like an igloo; and consider a time and place when this gatehouse may habe been used for ceremonial and/or security reasons. Take the dirt path to the left of the house and follow it for 300 feet. You will see what looks like an old dirt road heading toward the talus slope. Go along this road 150 feet to Stop 16, a huge Canyon Live Oak (see Shuttle Bus Stop 7 of Adventure 2 for a description of Canyon Live Oak). On the Valley floor, these trees are basically shrubs, but on bouldery slopes like the one behind the tree, they grow into trees rivalling the California Black Oak in size.

On the Valley wall side of this tree the trunk is nearly hollow; but still the tree survives with one huge limb. Notice that there is a charred trunk inside; my guess is that someone lit a campfire inside this tree. The boulders around the tree are covered with moss. The presence of moss indicates both that this is an area moist enough to provide the huge tree water, and that these boulders have been here a long time. The soil around these trees is dark and rich, with plenty of organic material. This is typical of soils in which Canyon Live Oak prospers in Yosemite Valley.

Go back down the dirt road and travel down the dirt path another 150 feet to Stop 17; to your left is a Ponderosa Pine with "old" bark (see Adventure 1); just ahead is a misshapen Ponderosa (at Stop 18) which has obviously had an eventful life. Just 100 feet down the path, cross the road and travel east on the asphalt path to the bus stop.

This is the end of Adventure 4, a trip through time, history and plants rare to the Valley.

ADVENTURE 5

On the Old Village Trail

In this adventure, we look at how man has used trees in building in the Valley: harvesting lumber from the native forest, planting yard trees for food and for beauty, and using existing trees in building plans. And because everything in the Valley is connected to everything else, we will explore a little about the geology, history and archeology of this area. There is no better place for this than the Old Village townsite, between Sentinel Bridge and the chapel.

This area was the center of Yosemite's action from the 1860s to the 1920s, but it has been "restored" — that is, the Park Service has removed 52 of the 53 frame buildings present in 1924. Nevertheless, there are many remnants of former activity (including trees planted by settlers), and the objective of this adventure is to find remnants and through them to consider the life of those days. There is a Treasure Map of the area with buildings identified by number in the envelope included with this Adventure. But you are going to need to bring your imagination too.

Get off the Shuttle Bus at Stop 11 and cross the newest Sentinel Bridge, descendant of the first bridge crossing the Merced River in the Valley. As you cross the bridge, look across the south Valley road at the two large old Incense Cedar trees with few leaves on the south side of the river. Head for the one to the right.

Just this side of the tree is the site of the second hotel built in the Valley, a building which housed guests from 1859 to 1941, and which is designated as Number 1 on the map. This building, originally called the Upper Hotel, had a dormitory for men on the first floor and for women on the second floor. It was built of wood sawn by hand, since there were no sawmills in the Valley then. The rooms had muslin sheets for partitions.

In 1864 the building was taken over by James Hutchings, the man who has done more to popularize Yosemite than anyone else. A disastrous flood in 1867 felled hundreds of pine and oak trees in the Valley, at the same time when Yosemite was becoming the thing to "do" in the eyes of the 19th-Century equivalent of the "Jet Set". Seeing a burgeoning tourist population which demanded creature comforts such as doors on hotel rooms, and having a huge supply of lumber, Hutchings added porches and interior walls to the hotel (which he called "Hutching's"). To do this, he built a sawmill and got a young man named John Muir to run it. As the 1870s wore on, the tourist population continued to grow, and improvements made the hotel more comfortable. Hutchings, Yosemite's answer to P. T. Barnum, enlarged the hotel around this Incense Cedar tree, which was probably 150 to 200 years old; now, in old age, it is about 300.

About 10 feet above the ground on the side of the tree away from the Chapel there are two rows of holes. These holes were created when the roof was nailed to the tree. On two rocks about 10 feet from the tree are bronze circles with inscriptions stating that these were corners of the "Big Tree Room". There are four more bronze circles in this immediate area, all on rocks within 50 feet of the tree. Two mark corners of this hotel, which was called "Cedar Cottage" when it was torn down by the CCC in 1941; the other two mark two corners of "Oak Cottage", another building in the Sentinel Hotel group (Number 2 on the map). Oak Cottage was built in 1898 and was torn down at about the same time as Cedar Cottage. None of these markers is at the exact location.

The two old Bigleaf Maple trees nearby were probably planted as yard trees between Cedar and Oak Cottages.

On the path toward the Chapel about 100 feet from the Big Tree, there is a clearing in the rocks. Hutchings, sensing the need for more accommodations, had "Rock Cottage" (Number 3) designed and built here in 1870. The motif was obviously a blend of building and rocks; for there are plenty of rocks around the Rock Cottage site.

The pioneer trying to build in the Old Village had two obstacles: trees and rocks. He could cut down the trees or build around them; he could build over rocks less than two feet high) by putting the building on stilts); but if they were higher he had to move them, blast them, chip them down to size or build around

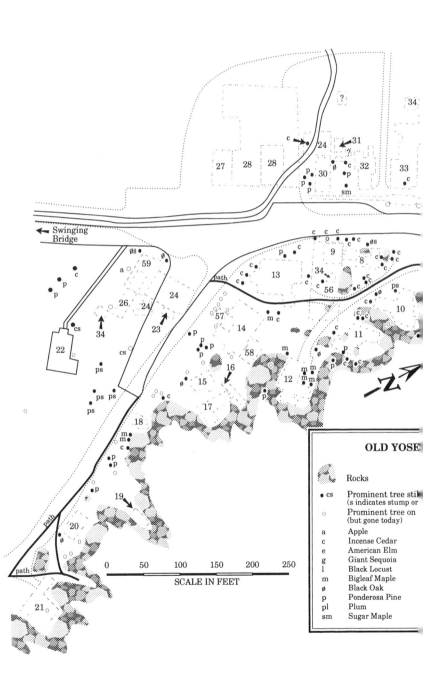

OLD YOSE

Rocks

• cs Prominent tree stil
      (s indicates stump or

○ Prominent tree on
      (but gone today)

a   Apple
c   Incense Cedar
e   American Elm
g   Giant Sequoia
l   Black Locust
m   Bigleaf Maple
ø   Black Oak
p   Ponderosa Pine
pl   Plum
sm   Sugar Maple

Swinging
Bridge

SCALE IN FEET
0   50   100   150   200   250

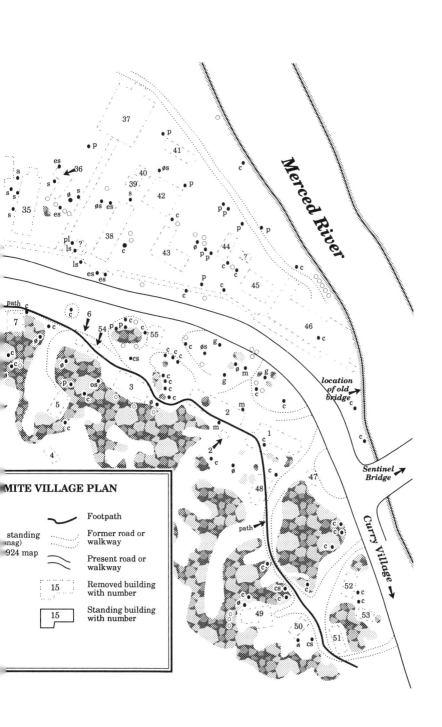

Merced River

37

• p

41

es •→ 36

a

s • s • s

s • ø

s 35 • es

38

40 • øs

39

42

• p

øs es

p

pl

ls ?

ls

es • es

• p

• c

• c

p p

• c

p

• p

43

ø

p p

44

c c

?

c

45

• c

p

c

path c

7

6

54 p p c c 55

c

c

c

c

c c c ø s g

cs

c c c

c c

c

ø

g

m

ø

g

3

p

os

c

c c c

ø

5

c

ø

m

2

m

4

c

2

c

ø

c

46

• c

location
of old
bridge c

• c

• c

• c

1

c

47

c

48

path

c

c

cs
c

c

49

50

ø cs

51

c
c

c

c

c

52
• c
• c

53

Sentinel
Bridge →

Curry Village →

[...]MITE VILLAGE PLAN

〜 Footpath

standing
(nag)
924 map

········· Former road or
walkway

〜〜 Present road or
walkway

[15] Removed building
with number

| 15 | Standing building
with number

them. And, as the Village grew to its maximum size of more than 50 frame buildings and more than 50 tent cabins, later builders had to deal with rocks and trees.

Because the rocks and trees were so important to early builders, I am including on the map the locations of trees shown on the 1924 map (many of which are still standing or are stumps) and locations of the large rockfields.

About 100 feet down the trail is a break in the rocks about 20 feet wide which goes back about 100 feet into the rocks and woods and opens up at the site of the stable (Number 5). I looked for signs of blasting, but I couldn't find any. See what you think; I think the pioneers used the natural topography for this building.

As you come out again, notice the Giant Sequoia tree directly ahead of you. This is the only large tree in the Old Village with no other big trees wihin 60 feet in any direction. This tree, possibly originally planted around 1875, even has a name: the "Native Son Sequoia"; early in this century the area around it was paved and a fence was put around it.

I suspect that this tree was a replacement because it is smaller than the three neighboring Giant Sequoias planted in 1890; but the original tree at this site may have been planted by a Mr. Stegman, who sold Sequoia seeds in a shop nearby, as a way of advertising his business. He sold his business in 1877 to a Mr. Sinning, who sold beautiful carvings from native trees until he died in 1889.

The site of Sinning's shop (which was taken over by the Sierra Club as a forerunner of LeConte Memorial from 1898 to 1903) is on the Chapel side of the large rock just south of the path with three iron eye bolts. These bolts held iron cables, probably to hitch horses next to the shop; they can be seen in Sierra Club photos of the building (Number 7). This building, about 20 feet square, probably fit very neatly into the recess in the large rock.

To the left of the path, just past the site of Sinning's, is an open area in the rocks which contained a National Park Service building (Number 8). An overlay of the building shape from a 1924 map of the Old Village on the pattern of the rocks shows that the building was shaped to fit exactly inside the rocky area. The pine stump you see was in front of the building.

Down a flat, 10-foot-wide pathway to the left about 100 feet is another recess in the rocks. This is shown on a 1924 map as the site of the U. S. Commisioner s residence in the early years of this century (Number 11).

Another 100 feet or so down this path is the site of a meat market, and the path was probably used as a driveway for the building (Number 12). This site has iron pipes, pieces of concerete slab, and other remnants. To the left of the building site is a group of Bigleaf Maples, probably planted as landscaping. The meat market was originally built in 1911 by a Mr. McCauley. He had a contract to sell meat to the Army, which administrated Yosemite Valley from 1906 to 1916. McCauley sold the business two years later. Within a couple of years, the building was sold again to a company called Desmond Park Company, which went bankrupt within a couple of years. Its assets were bought by the Yosemite Park Company which by 1924 owned 26 buildings in the Old Village alone. In 1925 the Park Service merged Yosemite Park Company and the Curry Camping Company into Yosemite Park and Curry Company. This case, and the case of the Stegman/ Sinning/Sierra Club building, are typical of situations in the Old Village, where businesses changed hands frequently.

Back up the old road about 150 feet is a pile of rocks on the left. Just past it the footpath leads to the west (toward the Chapel). This part of the path was the driveway for Degnan s Store (Number 13), which fronted on the main street of town and which is the forerunner for the Degnan Building in the New Village. As you pass the high voltage box, look to the left and a few feet away you will see part of a concrete slab. This is probably what remains of the State of California barn, which was torn down later; on this site was also the Wells Fargo office fronting on the main street. Another 30 feet and you pass a Bigleaf Maple tree, which looks like landscaping for the second house of the Degnan family (Number 14). This house was built around 1900 to replace their original house built in the shape of the rock recess around it in 1884 about 100 feet southeast of here (Number 17). The four Bigleaf Maples near the site of the original house may have been planted as yard trees.

As you walk toward the Chapel (Number 22) from the site of the old house, you will see some rocks near a large Incense Cedar tree. Two of these have iron rings and one has a spike sticking out of it. Look at these and you can see how iron rings and eyes were put into the granite. First, a spike was driven with a sledge hammer into the hard granite rock. With each few hammerings, the spike was probably knocked sideways with the sledgehammer to keep it loose and to widen the hole in the rock. When the hole was deep enough, a ring or eye bolt was cemented into the rock. Sometimes the spike got jammed in the hole; then the hole was abandoned and a new hole was started elsewhere. There are several places in the Old Village where these spikes remain.

A few feet down the path extending south from the Chapel parking lot there is a flat spot in the rocks which appears the exact size and shape of Johnny Finch's Blacksmith Shop (Building 18), a building on a 1925 auto map of the Valley.

The two apple trees in the front yard of the chapel were planted in the yards of either the first store in the Old Village, a photo studio, a movie studio or a woodworking shop (all of which were in this same area at one time or another). The oak tree on the corner of the church parking lot and the one-way road, and the dead oak snag to its west, were possibly at the front corners of a general store catering to the needs of campers from 1877 to 1900, with four different owners. The last owner, a Mr. Salter, moved his store across the street, and a new building known as "The Studio of the Three Arrows" (Number 25) was built on the site in 1903.

Across the road next to the bike path there is a concrete sidewalk laid before 1924. To the left of the three Ponderosa Pine trees near the west end of the sidewalk is the site of "Garibaldi's New Store" which changed hands and was enlarged before being torn down in 1959 (Number 28). In back of the three trees and across the bike path are an apple tree, an oak tree and a cedar tree. The apple was obviously planted as a yard tree for the photo studio next to it (Number 29), owned by a Mr. Boysen; the cedar tree and oak tree match up with recesses in the studio. It seems likely that the photographer, wanting to expand, had to either cut down these two trees or build around them, and chose the latter course.

Two non-native Sugar Maple trees were planted in the Boysen side yard around 1903. One has died, but the other, just a few feet from the sidewalk, annually delights visitors with its flaming orange and red leaves.

Along the sidewalk toward Sentinel Bridge is an area where the sidewalk is wider and the curb is raised. This is the site of theNPS Adminstration Building (Number 33). In front of the building you can see the remains of two kinds of non-native trees,

Black Locust and American Elm. Although the Park Service has been trying to eradicate these trees, the trees are tenacious; for example, look for clumps of thin woody stems around a circle of what appears to be sawdust. Although the stumps have been pulverized, these American Elm trees are sprouting from the stumps. Black Locusts are also sprouting from stumps. Both of these species are fast-growing too; a four-inch-wide stump may have only 10 rings.

Past the NPS Administration Building there is an apple tree about 100 feet away from the sidewalk. This tree was in the yard of Best's Studio (Number 35), which was founded here in 1902 and was moved to a new building in the New Village in 1926. The building here was torn down the same year. In 1972 Best's Studio was renamed "The Ansel Adams Gallery".

Toward the right of the apple tree is a low rock with an iron ring and a shallow depression. This rock appears to have been used for grinding California Black Oak acorns by Indians who lived on the site of the Old Village (in the rocks behind Cedar Cottage there is at least one other grinding rock with several depressions).

A few feet toward the bridge there is a plum tree about 15 feet from the sidewalk. This tree was a yard tree for the next building, which probably had the most different uses of any building in the Old Village. It was built in 1871 as the Cosmopolitan Saloon (Number 38), and was widely thought of as the only place in the Old Village with any class. The affluent leisure-class tourist of the 1870s and 1880s, accustomed to staying at luxury hotels, was usually disappointed in the rustic accomodations of Yosemite Valley. But here at the Cosmopolitan he or she could get a drink or a great bath, or could play billiards on these premises. The Cosmopolitan was shut down by the Yosemite Commissioners, probably in response to pressure from abstinence groups (in 1884!). Parts of it were used as the Yosemite Guardian's office, lodgings, employees' quarters, and a barber shop until 1932, when it burned down. The site of the Cosmopolitan is marked by the change in the direction of the sidewalk.

Left of the sidewalk about 100 feet closer to the bridge is an area with no large trees. This is the site of Ivy Cottage (Number 41), built around the turn of the century as the seventh and last unit of the Sentinel Hotel complex.

Where the sidewalk turns, just past the Incense Cedar, there is a rock with a bronze marker commemorating the site of River Cottage (Number 43), built in 1870. River Cottage was just west of the building next to older Sentinel Bridges, a hotel built in 1876 as the Yosemite Falls Hotel, and called in turn Yosemite Park Hotel and Sentinel Hotel (Number 44). It was torn down in 1938; the only signs of it today are the remains of a rock wall and square holes for porch columns in the concrete sidewalk.

From the site of the old bridge (torn down in 1993), go down the path next to the river, and look towards Yosemite Falls. A few feet from the bridge, Lower Yosemite Falls comes into view; 100 feet or so further it disappears again. This is no accident; apparently the trees near the Falls were cut down so that the Leisure Class Tourist of the late 1800s could view the Falls from the comfort and safety of the hotel veranda, rather than actually visiting them.

Walk back to the bridge and look across the road to where we started this Adventure. On the south side of the road, between the sites of the Sentinel Hotel and the Cedar and Oak Cottage is an area of rocks and trees. In the heyday of the Old Village this was a sort of lawn area, with a fence around some rocks, three large California Black Oak trees, some small Incense Cedar trees and three young Giant Sequoia trees (planted in 1890 for landscaping); in the years since the turn of the century, the Incense Cedars and Giant Sequoias have grown into trees over 100 feet tall, one of the oak trees has disappeared without a trace, and one of the oak trees has fallen across what was once a driveway (barely missing one of the Giant Sequoia trees). Books about the Valley's history usually have at least one photo of the Sentinel Hotel complex on both sides of the road, as well as the lawn area; taken from somewhere near the Cosmopolitan site, they provide an idealized picture of what the Old Village was like.

Yet today there are only remnants. What happened? The combination of dilapidated wooden buildings in a place where the snow piles deep and the sun barely shines during the winter; no room for growth between the rocks to the south, the river to the north and an easily-flooded meadow to the west; the traffic congestion caused by the automobile (which made Yosemite Valley much more accessible to middle-class vacationers); and construction of the luxurious Ahwahnee Hotel convinced the Park

Service to relocate their offices and concessions businesses else-where. This spelled the doom for the Old Village.

Accordingly, the Park Service started vacating and razing buildings in the Old Village in the 1920s. The flood of 1937 may have accelerated this razing: during the period from 1937 to 1941 most of the buildings were torn down, including all the Sentinel Hotel units. By 1981 all the buildings had been removed except the Chapel.

This short adventure just scratched the surface of what is on the Old Village site; its intent was to give you an appreciation for some of the early history of Yosemite Valley. There are many other artifacts and remnants of the bygone era which you can seek on your own. These are given in Appendix B.

ADVENTURE 6

The Biggest and Best in the Valley

This adventure is about finding the "Biggest and Best" — tallest, widest, oldest and most magnificent — trees of each kind in Yosemite Valley. At the end of this chapter is my own list of candidates, including directions to find them so you can check them out too; I'm also including a Treasure Map to help you.

But first, how does a tree become the "biggest"? It grew in a spot extremely favorable to its growth, lived longer than the other trees around it, or a combination of both. Not all trees live to a ripe old age; something usually kills them first. I can think of six main things that kill trees, and will apply them to Ponderosa Pines.

The first thing that kills trees is fire, either by burning the cambium (growing) layer or by heating the tree so hot that some of the water inside turns to steam and the tree dries out or explodes because of the tremendous pressure. For a tree to survive a fire, it either has to have wood that doesn't burn readily (like that of the Giant Sequoia) or bark thick enough to insulate the cambium against high temperatures. This means that an old, thick-barked Ponderosa has a better chance of fire survival than the young one next to it; and an old Ponderosa may have survived 20 or more forest fires.

The second thing that kills trees is lightning. A tree taller than any others around it is highly susceptible to lightning bolts, and so a tall tree by itself on top of a ridge would probably not get old. Also, there is luck involved; lightning could strike one Ponderosa and not touch one of the same height next to it.

The third thing that kills trees is lack of water. A tree with a long tap root which goes deep into a deep soil would be favored; pines generally have long tap roots, except that most of the Valley pines never develop this root. A tree which grew in a soil with little water-bearing capacity might have to dig deeply, and this might be seen in old Ponderosas which are smaller than the fast-growing young ones next to them, and which seem to have a much longer life expectancy.

The fourth thing that kills trees is lack of light. Sunlight provides the energy to make the tree's food, and a shaded tree is unlikely to grow old (Ponderosa seedlings surrounded by tall forest trees have a very low possibility of survival). An old tree as tall as those around it would not be at a disadvantage here.

The fifth thing that kills trees is pests. For example, many Ponderosa Pines have been killed in the last few years by *Fomes annosus*, or "root rot", a fungus which needs moisture to live. Ponderosas whose roots are wet a couple months of the year (because they are in soil with poor drainage or are too near the water table) are susceptible to this pest which cuts off the roots near ground level (thereby cutting off the water supply necessary to life).

The sixth thing that kills trees is wind (or snow). "Mono Winds", periodically coming from the desert to the east of the Park, are funneled into the Valley, and topple trees with their great velocities. Trees weakened by root rot are often victims, because they are like a pencil (the trunk) with a sail on top (the leaves). Many Ponderosas next to the Merced River are killed by this lethal combination.

The monarchs on my list have so far withstood all these threats. Although there may be larger trees in the deep forest, those I selected are easily accessible (that is, within 100 feet from a road or trail).

I have measured each of these trees for "dbh" (short for "diameter at breast height", obtained by dividing the circumference at 4.5 feet by pi); height (measured with a clinometer, a standard tool used by foresters); spread (the horizontal extent of the leaves, paced off for the broadleaved trees only); and age of the stumps (by ring counts).

"Largest in the Sierra" is defined as the largest Sierra tree of each species cited in the literature. "Champions" are defined by the American Forestry Association as the largest tree of each species in the U. S. The champion trees were apparently selected for their diameters rather than their heights, so I'm giving dbh first for those. This list is current up to 1980.

One more thing: many of these trees are old and have a short life expectancy; so some may be gone by the time you read this book. Nevertheless, let's go for it!

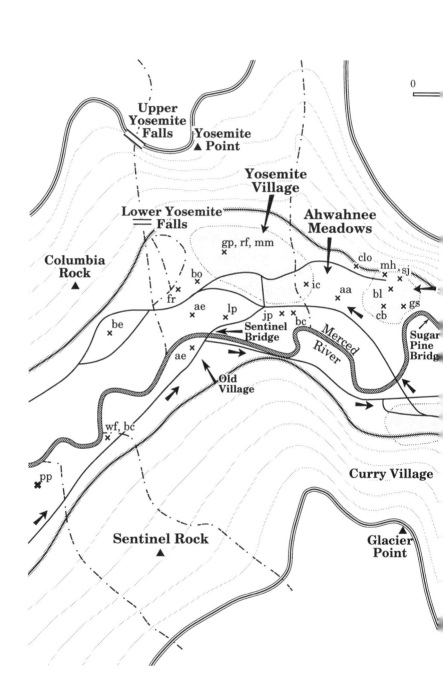

Upper Yosemite Falls

Yosemite ▲ Point

Yosemite Village

Lower Yosemite Falls

Ahwahnee Meadows

Columbia Rock ▲

gp, rf, mm ×

clo ×
mh · sj
bo ×
× ic
aa ×
bl ×
× gs
fr ×
ae ×
lp ×
jp × ×
cb ×
be ×
bc ·
Sentinel Bridge
Merced River
ae ×
Old Village
Sugar Pine Bridge

wf, bc ×

Curry Village

pp ×

Sentinel Rock ▲

Glacier Point ▲

0

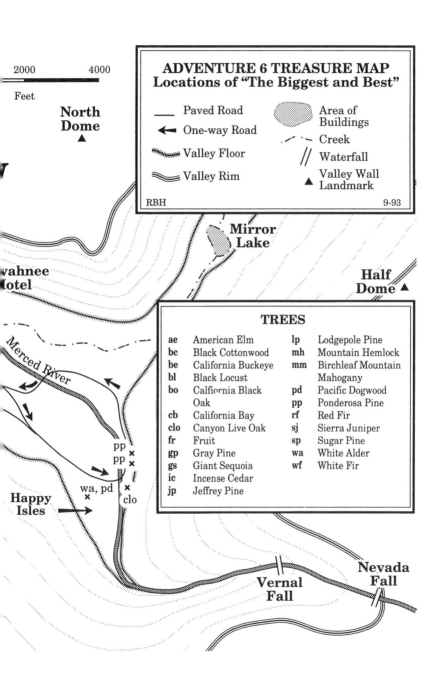

2000   4000

Feet

**North
Dome**
▲

**ADVENTURE 6 TREASURE MAP
Locations of "The Biggest and Best"**

—— Paved Road

◄— One-way Road

〰〰 Valley Floor

〰〰 Valley Rim

Area of Buildings

.-⁓-. Creek

// Waterfall

▲ Valley Wall Landmark

RBH   9-93

**Mirror
Lake**

**Half
Dome** ▲

**wahnee
otel**

Merced River

**Happy
Isles** ➤

pp ×
pp ×

wa, pd ×

clo

TREES

ae	American Elm	lp	Lodgepole Pine
bc	Black Cottonwood	mh	Mountain Hemlock
be	California Buckeye	mm	Birchleaf Mountain
bl	Black Locust		Mahogany
bo	Calfiornia Black Oak	pd	Pacific Dogwood
		pp	Ponderosa Pine
cb	California Bay	rf	Red Fir
clo	Canyon Live Oak	sj	Sierra Juniper
fr	Fruit	sp	Sugar Pine
gp	Gray Pine	wa	White Alder
gs	Giant Sequoia	wf	White Fir
ic	Incense Cedar		
jp	Jeffrey Pine		

**Nevada
Fall**

**Vernal
Fall**

Native to the Valley; conditions are favorable for optimum growth

Ponderosa Pine:

Tallest: "Grandma", on the right edge of the Shuttle Bus Loop between Stops 16 and 17 of Adventure 2, a few hundred yards from Happy Isles Bridge; 250 feet tall and 5.9 feet dbh.

Thickest and Most Magnificent: "Grandpa", on the right edge of the road 200 feet before "Grandma"; 230 feet tall and 6.0 feet dbh.

Oldest Stump: Along the north bank of the Merced River alongside the dirt path between the Happy Isles and Mirror Lake shuttle bus stops; 298 years, with a maximum diameter of 4.5 feet. A Valley stump was reported in the literature at 407 years.

Largest in the Sierra: In Yellow Pine Sentinel Beach Picnic Ground, next to the road through the picnic area, a fallen trunk 80 feet long and about 6 feet in diameter. This tree was reported by John Muir as a standing giant 210 feet high and 8 feet in diameter, and was a Valley tourist attraction until it fell in the 1930s. My tree ring count of the non-rotted wood is 260 years, measured 75 feet from the base of the tree; but it would have taken the tree about 30 years or so to reach this height, so I estimate the tree at 300 years plus.

Champion: The widest, near Lapine, Oregon, is 8.6 feet dbh and 162 feet tall. The tallest, in Shasta-Trinity National Forest, is 262 feet tall and 5.3 feet dbh.

Douglas Fir:

Tallest and Widest: On the left edge of the south Valley road, 1.2 miles past the Bridal Veil Falls (Highway 41) turnoff; 190 feet tall and 7.3 feet dbh. Honorable Mention goes to the tree on the southeast corner of Pohono Bridge, 180 feet tall and 6.5 feet dbh.

Largest in the Sierra: This tree is large for the Sierra, but Douglas Firs in the Cascade Range in Washington and Oregon grow much larger: a tree cut as a flagpole for a 1915 exposition was reportedly 299 feet tall.

Champion: In Olympic National Park, Washington, 14.5 feet dbh, 221 feet tall.

White Fir:

Tallest and Widest: On the Merced riverbank a few yards upstream from Swinging Bridge, hidden among other trees; 185 feet tall and 5.5 feet dbh.

Oldest Stump: In front of LeConte Memorial (Shuttle Bus Stop 12 in Adventure 2), 129 years and 2.2 feet in diameter.

Largest in the Sierra and Champions: In Sierra National Forest, over 8.0 feet dbh and 180 feet tall; near Merced Lake in Yosemite, 8.3 feet dbh; tallest champion, 213 feet high and 7.0 feet dbh in Plumas National Forest; widest champion, 8.8 feet dbh and 179 feet tall near Mt. Diablo, California.

Incense Cedar:

Tallest: No one tree dominates this category, but the tallest I have seen is a 165-foot tree in the Tecoya Employee Housing Area (location shown on Adventure 1 Treasure Map).

Widest and Most Magnificent: At the edge of the parking lot at Swinging Bridge Picnic Ground, on the south Valley road; 130 feet tall and 7.6 feet dbh. This tree has another claim to fame: Galen Clark built a cabin beneath it.

Oldest Stump: Along the north Valley road, between El Capitan Meadow and Pohono Bridge, on the north side of the road as you go down one of the hills on this stretch; about 400 years and 5.2 feet in diameter. (Park at the Bridal Veil Fall viewpoint, V10 in *The Yosemite Road Guide* , and walk back about 100 yards uphill to the stump)

Champions: Widest, near Rouge River, California, 11.5 feet dbh; tallest, in Umpqua National Forest, Oregon, 225 feet tall and 5.2 feet dbh.

Black Cottonwood:

Tallest: A double-trunked tree in the forest about 20 feet left (south) of the North one-way road just west of Ahwahnee Meadow (location shown on Adventure 1 Treasure Map); 110 feet tall, 3.4 feet dbh, 25 foot spread.

Widest: Next to the south side of Swinging Bridge; 100 feet tall, 3.8 feet dbh, 65 foot spread.

Largest Stump: A double stump next to the road near the tallest tree is 2.5 feet in diameter at 100 years.

Champion: Near Haines, Alaska, 10.4 feet dbh, 101 feet tall, 60 foot spread.

Willow:

Tallest, Widest and Biggest Spread: No single tree stands out; typically old willows are 30 to 50 feet tall, 3 feet dbh, 30 foot spread.

White Alder:

Tallest, Widest and Biggest Spread: Standing by itself on the dirt path from Bus Stop 16 to the Happy Isles Nature Center, about 150 feet past the rest rooms; 120 feet tall, 2.5 feet dbh, 50 foot spread.

Largest in the Sierra and Champion: In Angeles National Forest, 3.6 feet dbh and 93 feet tall, 45 foot spread.

California Black Oak:

Tallest and Widest: 100 feet north of the bike path between the Village and Yosemite Creek, where the bike path turns to the left (location shown on Adventure 7 Treasure Map); 130 feet tall, 5.9 feet dbh, 75 foot spread.

Biggest Spread: About 150 feet east of the above tree, has a metal tag with "130" on it; 105 feet tall, 5.0 feet dbh, 110 foot spread.

Oldest Stump: On south side of the Shuttle Bus route, between Stops 4 and 5, opposite the Medical Clinic entrance, halfway between the road to the Ahwahnee Hotel and employee housing (location indicated on Adventure 1 Treasure Map); 330 years.

Largest in the Sierra and Champion: In Pate Valley, Yosemite National Park, 11.5 feet dbh, height and spread not given.

Canyon Live Oak:

Tallest: On the right (south) side of the Shuttle Bus Loop just past the Happy Isles Bridge between Shuttle Bus Stops 16 and 17; 105 feet high, 3.9 feet dbh, 80 foot spread.

Widest: Near the road from the Village to the Ahwahnee Hotel (Stop 16 of Adventure 4); 5.8 feet dbh, 60 feet tall with a spread of 48 feet.

Largest in the Sierra and Champion: In Cleveland National Forest, California, 10.8 feet dbh, 72 feet tall, 97 foot spread.

California Bay:

Tallest, Widest and Biggest Spread: Next to the Ahwahnee Hotel (Stop 6 of Adventure 4); 32 feet tall, four trunks (the largest is 0.5 feet dbh) with a spread of 22 feet.

Champion: Near the Rogue River, Oregon; 13.3 feet dbh, 88 feet tall, 70 foot spread.

Bigleaf Maple:

  Tallest, Widest and Biggest Spread: No tree stands out, but my candidate is a tree in the yard of the former Degnan Residence in the Old Village (see Adventure 5 Treasure Map); 75 feet tall, 1.2 feet dbh, 24 foot spread.
  Champion: On San Juan Island, Washington, 7.8 feet dbh, 98 feet tall, 104 foot spread.

Pacific Dogwood:

  Tallest, Widest and Biggest Spread: On the dirt path between Shuttle Bus Stop 16 and Happy Isles Nature Center, about 50 yards past the rest rooms; 55 feet tall, 1.0 feet dbh, 33 foot spread.
  Champion: Tacoma, Washington, 2.9 feet dbh, 60 feet tall, 42 foot spread.

Native to the Valley Rim (but planted here naturally); conditions are okay but not optimum

Sugar Pine:

  Thickest and Most Magnificent: At Sugar Pine Bridge, on the east bank of the Merced River (Stop 12 of Adventure 4); 185 feet tall and 8.1 feet dbh. Tree ring cores indicate an age of about 360 years.
  Tallest: On the right side of the road just past Pohono Bridge; 190 feet tall and 5.9 feet dbh.
  Largest in Sierra and Champion: The tallest reported (in 1992) is in the woods just south of Hodgdon Meadow, and is 270 feet high. The widest reported in the literature was a blowndown tree 18 feet dbh and 245 feet long. The champion, in Standard, Calfornia, is 10.2 feet dbh and 230 feet high.

Jeffrey Pine:

Tallest and Widest: On the left (south) edge of the north Valley road about 100 yards before the right turn to the Village, near the employee tent cabins (better location on Adventure 1 Treasure Map); 165 feet tall and 4.4 feet dbh. You will have to smell for this one!

Largest in the Sierra and Champion: In Sierra National Forest, 7.3 feet dbh and 182 feet tall.

Lodgepole Pine:

Tallest and Widest: On the right (north) side of the road halfway between Shuttle Bus Stops 10 and 11. This tree is 80 feet tall and 1.7 feet dbh (but if you cross the road and stomp around in the woods you will find a grove of larger ones, the largest of which is a dead tree 95 feet tall and 2.6 feet dbh).

Largest in the Sierra and Champion: In Stanislaus National Forest, 6.7 feet dbh and 91 feet tall.

Red Fir:

Tallest: In the Museum Garden (Stop 26 of Adventure 3); 60 feet tall and 0.7 feet dbh; but trees at the elevation of the Valley Rim are commonly 150 feet tall and over 4 feet dbh.

Largest in the Sierra and Champion: At Glacier Point, 186 feet tall and 7 feet dbh before it fell during a storm; the champion is in Lassen Volcanic National Park, 168 feet tall and 8.1 feet dbh.

Not native to the Valley; had to be planted, so no "big, old" trees

Gray Pine:

Tallest and Widest: In the Museum Garden (Stop 1 of Adventure 3); 55 feet tall and 0.9 feet dbh.
Largest in the Sierra and Champion: Near Coalinga, Fresno County, 5.0 feet dbh and 155 feet tall.

Knobcone Pine:

Tallest and Widest: In the NPS residential area (see Adventure 7 Treasure Map for better location); 80 feet tall, 4.0 feet dbh.
Largest in the Sierra and Champion: The official AFA champion is 3.3 feet dbh and 98 feet tall. I have proposed our tree as new champion.

Mountain Hemlock:

Tallest and Widest: Beside the Ahwahnee Hotel pond (see Adventure 4 for better location); 42 feet tall and 1.1 feet dbh.
Largest in the Sierra and Champion: In Stanislaus National Forest, California, 6.0 feet dbh, 118 feet tall.

Giant Sequoia:

Tallest and Widest: On the eastern edge of the Ahwahnee Hotel lawn (Stop 18 of Adventure 4); 195 feet tall and 7.3 feet dbh.
Largest in the Sierra and Champions: Widest, "General Sherman", in Sequoia National Park, California, 26.7 feet diameter at 10 feet above the ground and 272 feet tall; tallest, a tree in Redwood Mountain Grove, Sequoia National Park, reported to be 310 feet tall; oldest stump authenticated by ring count, nearly 3200 years.

Sierra Juniper:

Tallest and Widest: Next to the Ahwahnee pond (see Adventure 4 for better location); 42 feet tall and 0.7 feet dbh.

Largest in the Sierra and Champion: Across Tioga Road from Tenaya Lake, up to 10 feet dbh; the champion, in Stanislaus National Forest, is 13.0 feet dbh and 87 feet tall.

Quaking Aspen:

Tallest, Widest and Most Magnificent: In Ahwahnee Meadow, 200 feet north of the north Valley road; the "mother" tree of this grove is 85 feet tall, 3.3 feet dbh, 40 foot spread; none of the numerous "babies" is more than 60 feet tall or 0.7 feet dbh.

Champion: Near Santa Fe, New Mexico, 3.7 feet dbh, 70 feet tall, 45 foot spread.

California Buckeye:

Tallest, Widest and Biggest Spread: In front of Cedar Cottage at Yosemite Lodge; 24 feet tall; biggest trunk, 0.5 feet dbh, 22 foot spread.

Champion: Near Olema, California, 4.1 foot dbh, 35 feet tall, 40 foot spread.

American Elm:

Tallest, Widest, Biggest Spread and Most Magnificent: In Cook's Meadow north of Sentinel Bridge, about 300 feet south of the north Valley road; 80 feet tall, 2.9 feet dbh, 93 foot spread.

Largest Stump: Sprouts from a removed stump in front of the Cosmopolitan Saloon site in the Old Village indicate the tree may have been up to 4 feet dbh at about 120 years (see Adventure 5).

Champion: Louisville, Kansas, 7.4 feet dbh, 99 feet tall, 133 foot spread.

Black Locust:

Tallest and Biggest Spread: In the loading dock area of the Ahwahnee Hotel (see Adventure 4 for better location); 105 feet tall, 2.7 feet dbh, 75 foot spread.
Widest: Next to the above tree; 95 feet tall and 3.1 feet dbh.
Champion: Near Jefferson, Indiana, 5.1 feet dbh, 85 feet tall with a 60 foot spread.

Fruit Tree:

Tallest, Widest and Biggest Spread: The largest cherry tree is in the Schoolyard Orchard between the Village and Yosemite Lodge (100 feet from where a bike path splits off to the north from the main path, then about 50 feet to the left); this tree has a metal tag with "26" on it and is not shaped like any other tree in the orchard; 55 feet tall, 2.9 feet dbh, 33 foot spread. No apple tree in the Valley dominates in size; typically apple trees are about 40 feet tall, 1.5 to 2.0 feet dbh, 35 foot spread. The widest apple tree I found was in the Curry Village orchard, with a metal tag with "99" on it; 50 feet tall, 2.6 feet dbh, 33 foot spread.

Adventure 6. has taken us all over theValley, but what a reward! We have seen some of the biggest and best-looking trees here.

ADVENTURE 7

In Search of the Giant Sequoias

In this adventure, with the aid of my directions and a Treasure Map, you will try to find all 47 Giant Sequoia trees growing in the Valley.

So why do I think there are only 47? The answer lies in characteristics of the Giant Sequoias of Yosemite. They grow naturally in the three groves of the Park, but none of these is upstream from the Valley, so seeds could not float into the Valley. And the nearest grove is about 10 miles from the Valley, so there is no way the wind could carry the seeds. Speaking of seeds, one author stated that the chance of a Giant Sequoia seed developing into a mature tree is one billion to one, so those cones you see on the ground around Giant Sequoias in this Adventure have very little chance of reproducing the species. (A fun activity is to look around the mature trees for Giant Sequoia seedlings. I have seen many in the Park's three groves, but not one in the Valley)

How did these 47 trees get here? They were transplanted. Since Giant Sequoias are apparently difficult to transplant, probably many more were originally planted — some as part of landscaping plans, some as yard trees.

Once they establish themselves, these trees grow about as rapidly in both height and width as the Ponderosas. One report in the Yosemite Research Library documents the size of Giant Sequoias in Europe, which were planted starting around 1855. Of several hundred trees listed, the tallest is 143 feet, about the average of our 47 trees; however, the widest listed tree (growing in Spain) is 13 feet wide, much wider than anything in the Valley. Another report documents the size of some trees in Wawona; apparently trees of the same age are taller in Yosemite Valley than in the other places.

Speaking of age, I don't know the exact planting date of most of the Giant Sequoias in the Valley (because landscapers almost never document the plantings of trees); but I'm going to make my best guesses as to date of planting, so that you can envision how quickly they may have grown. I'm also giving my measurements of tree sizes.

To find the 47 trees, go to the following areas:

Ahwahnee Hotel Grounds (25 trees): Seven trees are around the tennis court, and 11 trees are growing in a line in the parking lot of the hotel (see Shuttle Bus Stop 4). There are also four more trees around the parking lot (one is near the pond). All these trees were probably planted between 1926 and 1930, during or right after hotel construction.

Two more trees are on the front lawn of the hotel, and another is on the edge of the front lawn on the bank of Royal Arch Creek (the "Ahwahnee Tree"). These trees were possibly planted around 1888 by William Coffman, who operated stables on the Ahwahnee Hotel site.

The "Ahwahnee Tree" no doubt has been pampered by generations of gardeners. It is still "young" (possible planting date 1888), but it is a marvelous specimen at 195 feet tall and 7.3 feet in diameter.

All the Ahwahnee area trees are indicated on the Adventure 4 Treasure Map.

Old Village Area (eight trees): Three are in an area on the south side of the south Valley road about 200 feet west of Sentinel Bridge. These three, planted in 1890, average 150 feet high and 5 feet in diameter. Another tree, called the "Native Son Sequoia", is 200 feet farther toward the chapel on the south side of the road; a man who sold Sequoia seeds nearby may have planted a tree there originally around 1875; but the fact that this tree is smaller than the three nearby trees suggests that it may have been a replacement tree. These trees are indicated on the Adventure 5 Treasure Map.

Another tree is growing right next to an old apple tree about 100 feet west of the Chapel. This tree is now higher than the apple tree, and will eventually kill the apple tree. It is probably younger than the other four trees in the Old Village area.

There are three trees near Sentinel Bridge. One tree is next to the road northeast of the bridge, and there was some concern about the impact of the bridge on this tree's life expectancy. Two smaller trees are in the woods a few feet east of this tree (go down the stairway built into the bridge and you will see them); they were planted next to Chris Jorgensen's cabin sometime after 1900.

Curry Village Area (one tree): This tree is in the front yard of Mother Curry's Bungalow, and it is not a particularly big tree. It was planted after 1928.

Yosemite Village Area (11 trees): In the National Park Service residential area, inside a loop street, there are three trees, probably planted about 1915. Centered about the Yosemite Museum are four more trees: one is on the south side of the Ranger's Club (planted about 1920), one is a few feet to the right as you walk out of the Museum (planted about 1926), and two are in the garden behind the museum (planted in 1936). In the Pioneer Cemetary there are five trees Galen Clark planted near his future grave about 1896; apparently he planted around a dozen, but the rest died. These 11 trees are indicated on the Treasure Map included with this Adventure.

Yosemite Creek Area (one tree): On the north Valley road just to the east of the bridge over Yosemite Creek, there is a driveway leading to a National Park Service building. Two hundred feet toward the building is a tree called "The Superintendent's Tree". This tree is 180 feet tall, 6.6 feet in diameter; it was planted around 1915.

The next two pages give my measurements of Giant Sequoias in the Valley. Happy hunting in Adventure 7!

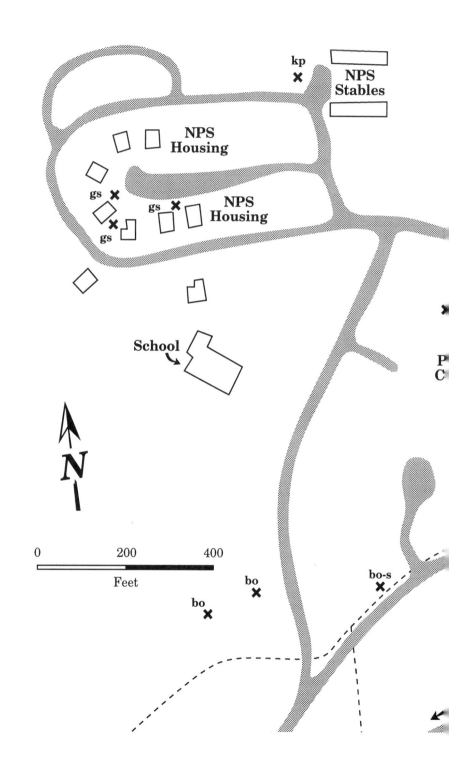

kp

NPS
Stables

NPS
Housing

gs

gs

gs

NPS
Housing

School

N

0   200   400

Feet

bo

bo

bo-s

P
C

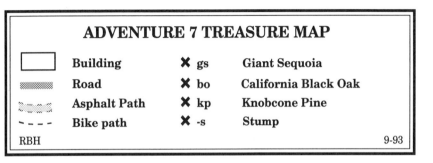

ADVENTURE 7 TREASURE MAP

	Building	✘ gs	Giant Sequoia
	Road	✘ bo	California Black Oak
	Asphalt Path	✘ kp	Knobcone Pine
- - -	Bike path	✘ -s	Stump

RBH   9-93

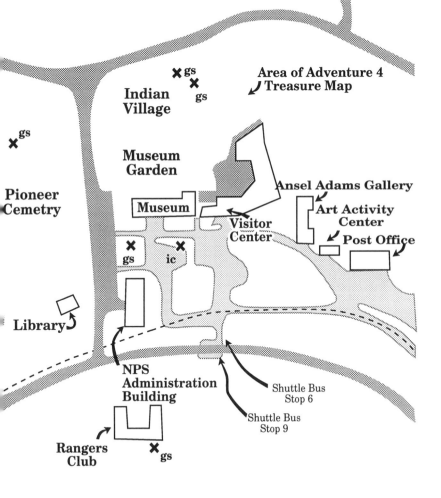

Indian Village

Area of Adventure 4 Treasure Map

Museum Garden

Pioneer Cemetery

Museum

Ansel Adams Gallery

Art Activity Center

Visitor Center

Post Office

Library

NPS Administration Building

Shuttle Bus Stop 6

Shuttle Bus Stop 9

Rangers Club

to Yosemite Lodge

Location	Designation	Est. Date Planted	Girth (in.)	Width (in.)	Height (ft)
Ahwahnee	Front Lawn 1	1888	146	3.9	100
"	" " 2	1888	164	4.4	90
"	Ahwahnee Tree	1888	276	7.3	195
"	Parking Lot 1	1927	181	4.1	160
"	" " 2	1927	148	3.9	160
"	" " 3	1927	101	2.7	140
"	" " 4	1927	135	3.6	145
"	" " 5	1927	164	4.4	145
"	" " 6	1927	142	3.8	150
"	" " 7	1927	127	3.4	125
"	" " 8	1927	136	3.6	145
"	" " 9	1927	155	4.1	150
"	" " 10	1927	148	3.9	150
"	" " 11	1927	102	2.7	105
"	" " 12	1927	148	3.9	115
"	" " 13	1927	170	4.5	130
"	" " 14	1927	155	4.1	120
"	Pond	1927	125	3.3	110
"	Tennis Court 1	1927	178	4.7	150
"	" " 2	1927	170	4.5	140
"	" " 3	1927	151	4.0	150
"	" " 4	1927	145	3.8	150
"	" " 5	1927	98	2.6	115
"	" " 6	1927	76	2.0	110
"	" " 7	1927	95	2.5	100
Curry	Mother Curry	After 1928	50	1.3	65

Location	Designation	Est. Date Planted	Girth (in.)	Width (in.)	Height (in.)
Old Village	Chapel Tree	Before 1903	72	1.9	70
"	Native Son	1875?	145	3.8	110
"	Sentinel Hotel 1	1890	190	5.0	135
"	" " 2	1890	167	4.4	140
"	" " 3	1890	196	5.2	145
"	Sentinel Bridge	After	135	3.6	150
"	Jorgensen 1	1900	31	0.8	37
"	" 2	"	80	2.1	90
"					
Yos. Village	Cemetary 1	1896	129	3.4	145
"	Cemetary 2	1896	61	1.6	90
"	Cemetary 3	1896	135	3.6	155
"	Cemetary 4	1896	88	2.3	140
"	Cemetary 5	1896	123	3.3	150
"	Mus. Garden 1	1936	79	2.1	80
"	" " 2	1936	31	0.8	32
"	Mus. Front	1926	185	4.9	150
"	Rangers Club	1920	228	6.0	140
NPS Area	Res. Area 1	1915	200	5.3	135
" "	" " 2	1915	220	5.8	130
" "	" " 3	1915	139	3.7	125
Yos. Creek	Supt's. Tree	1915	250	6.6	165

ADVENTURE 8

Tree Adventures All Year

Although many of Yosemite Valley's visitors come during June, July and August, people come here all year. Each month the trees of the Valley are doing something different: even during the winter months, dormant-looking broadleaved trees are doing something. In this adventure, we'll look at some things of interest for any month you are here.

The descriptions and sketches oother Adventures may help you identify specific trees.

January

Typically the Valley floor is covered with snow. Snow in the Sierra is wet, and if it falls with little or no wind, it sticks to tree branches and leaves. If it snows while you are here, you are likely in for quite a treat: Sometimes after an overnight snow, the conifers look like flocked Christmas trees, and the bare horizontal branches of the broadleaved trees have an inch or two of snow on top of them. This spectacle is great not only for photographers, but for anyone else with an eye for peace and beauty. Typically after the storm the clouds disappear and the sky turns Yosemite Blue once again. This, and the cool crisp air, make you feel great to be alive.

After the storm the sun starts to melt the snow, and globs of snow drop off the branches, you start wishing for another storm.

Although this is not the best month to identify broadleaved trees and shrubs, you can identify eight fairly easily. California Bay and Canyon Live Oak keep most of their leaves all winter; California Black Oak leaves turn brown and die but may stay on the tree all winter; Pacific Dogwood has round flower buds with four to six little triangles; White Alder has tiny "cones" and "caterpillars" in its bare branches; Quaking Aspen has almost-white bark and no "cones"; Creek Dogwood has maroon to red twigs on the end of its branches; and Spice Bush has brown seed cases. You can find good examples of all these either around the Village Store or along the Village Pedestrian Mall (again, please refer to other Adventures for specific trees or shrubs).

February

February is almost like January, except that the "caterpillars" of the White Alders are larger and have turned green; they are now more obvious than the "cones". A good place to look is in front of the Yosemite Lodge Registration Building.

Check out the area around the base of the trees. It amazed me at first to see circles of bare ground around the Ponderosas and Incense Cedars but no circles around the California Black Oaks in the same area. It may be that the oaks are not melting the snow around their bases (that is, using water and growing) and the other trees are. There may also be other reasons. This is something I plan to explore in the future.

March

The buds of various trees have grown between February and March, and the trees are getting ready to burst forth with flowers or leaves in April.

Snow probably still covers the ground, but there is as much rain as snow now. Both keep moisture in the ground, which will help the trees survive the long dry Sierra Summer.

A fun activity starting in late March is to look for the first trees in an area with leaves appearing; in fact, the first time I did this I checked every few days to see how soon I could identify specific trees. Landscaped areas are the best places to do this, because they have the greatest variety of trees and shrubs.

California Buckeye is unusual because it is often the first tree to leaf out in the Spring (usually in late March) and the first tree whose leaves turn brown (usually in August).

This month California Bay has small but pretty white blooms.

April

The Valley trees have finally made it through winter and their buds are opening this month. Everywhere you look there is fresh light green growth. Pick a few trees, one of each kind, in your lodging area or the Village; if you are here for a couple days, look each day at new leaves which unfolded the day before. At last you can identify the different trees by their leaves; but bear in mind that the earliest leaves are smaller and maybe slightly differently shaped than later ones.

Look at the future flowers of a Pacific Dogwood tree. The triangles sticking out from the round flower buds seem to be a little longer each day, and are developing into petals.

The Bigleaf and Dwarf Maples have flowers this month, but they are about the only trees that do, except for the non-native apples and pears. Fruit trees have many beautiful blooms in April, and the best places to look for apple blossoms are in the three orchards in the Valley; the plum tree in the Old Village (see Adventure 5 for location) is also loaded with white blooms.

Conifers also show new light green growth. Ponderosa Pines are extremely interesting this month, because the new growth is not only up but also out, usually in four directions from the top. By the end of the year these short twigs may have grown a foot.

May

This is the most wonderful month for flowers in the Valley. The Pacific Dogwood "petals" (actually specialized leaves) have been lengthening and turning from yellow green to almost white; now they overlap and make a beautiful bloom. Note one thing, though; the flower buds grow at different rates in each tree, even though all trees are of one single species.

One thing I like doing is searching for the Pacific Dogwood tree with the most flowers, because some are loaded with flowers and some have few or none. My favorite places for comparison are the Ahwahnee Hotel area, the Curry Village area and the yards on the west side of Ahwahnee Meadow. If you look at a few trees you will notice that, although all the trees are of the same species, some bloom later than others.

Evergreen broadleaved trees such as California Bay and Canyon Live Oak have had leaves all winter, but their new growth is also lighter in color and healthier-looking.

This month you may notice haze in the air and a yellowish powder which gets all over everything. This is Ponderosa Pine pollen, and it falls for a couple of weeks. Since there are so many Ponderosas in the Valley; since it sometimes rains in May; and since the pollen floats; there is usually a thick coating of yellow in wet areas.

June

Flowers are continuing this month, notably Western Azalea and Pacific Dogwood; but now Blue Elderberry starts blooming. The beauty of the flowers helps to offset the discomfort of hot cloudless days and the lack of rain (less than 3 percent of the annual Sierra precipitation falls during the summer).

This month seeds start to form, and show the contrast between seeds of trees otherwise similar. There are two cases for you to check out. The first is the maples. Bigleaf Maple has a stalk with several "samaras" (those winged seed cases), but typically Dwarf Maples have only a single pair of samaras on a stalk. Each Pacific Dogwood flower is starting to evolve into a cluster with a number of berries touching each other; each Creek Dogwood flower evolves into a single berry as separate as the flowers were.

If you go to a Black Cottonwood tree this month you will see why it is called "cottonwood": the tree sheds large quantities of what looks like cotton. This "cotton", formed arund the seeds, helps wind and water disperse the seeds, but it makes a mess around large trees at this point.

July

This month a whole different set of plants is blooming. The beautiful white and pink flowers of dogwoods and azaleas are gone, but in their place are the fragrant white flowers of Mock Orange and the fragrant red-brown flowers of Spice Bush. The Museum Garden and the Aspen Cottage area of Yosemite Lodge are both good places to smell these two types of flowers.

August

This month greets us with another set of colors. Fruits and seedpods are ripening on dogwood, Blue Elderberry, wild berries and Chokecherry. These plants apparently have colorful fruits so that animals can spot them, eat the tasty fruits and disperse the seeds by passing them through their digestive tracts. We humans know when the berries are ripe and tasty by their colors too. Besides, the colors are pleasing to our eyes.

There are other color changes too. The leaves of the California Buckeye are starting to turn yellow, showing us that Fall is coming. Maple samaras (seed cases) are turning brown, in contrast to the still bright green leaves.

A few Incense Cedar cones are falling this month, indicating that the conifers are changing too. Since these are so small and so few you may have to look under a few large trees to find the cones. They look like miniature fleur-de-lis an inch or less long (look at the sketch in Adventure 1). The best trees to look under are large trees which are not yet old. Look along the bike path near Aspen and Dogwood Cottages of Yosemite Lodge.

September

The most interesting thing to me this month is that a lot of the trees are starting to look "sick". The Ponderosas, Incense Cedars and even Giant Sequoias have brown needles among the deep green ones. Quaking Aspen and Black Cottonwood leaves have ugly-looking black and yellow areas, and the leaves are sticky and glossy; they appear to be sick. Remember that this is just the trees going through their cycles, and very few of the trees are actually in trouble.

Some of the forest trees may actually be dead or dying: the entire forest has gone through three months of hot weather with little or no rainfall. If a tree hasn't gotten enough water from its root system, it will die. Anywhere in the Valley or on the Valley Walls you look there are a few totally brown conifers. These trees are dead, but it's just part of the whole grand scheme.

California Buckeye, the leader for the rest of the trees, now has brown leaves, and they are falling. It also has green fruits which will turn brown and fall during Winter. But it shows that things are changing; the days are still hot (though not as hot as July or August) but the nights are getting cool. And this month you know that Winter is coming.

October

Congratulations! You are here in the most picturesque and colorful month of the Valley's year. Don't waste your time looking for water in the now-waterless Yosemite Falls; the trees are too glorious this month.

Every day this month things change. For example, the maples start the month with green leaves tinged with yellow; they finish the month with every color from green to yellow to orange to red to brown.

Wait a minute, how come these trees are changing color? And what is the "right" color? The answer lies in the process of color changes in leaves. First of all, leaves are green most of the year because the green chlorophyll in the leaves masks yellow and orange pigments. As Fall approaches, the tree starts to kill the cells at the base of the leaf, the chlorophyll breaks down and loses some of its green color, and the yellow and orange pigments show. As this process goes on, the leaf essentially dies of thirst and shrivels. The leaf falls when the connection to the twig is so weak that the twig no longer has enough strength to hold onto the leaf. (That is why a lot of leaves fall when the wind blows: the extra force exerted is enough to break the fragile connection.)

That explains the yellows, oranges and browns. Why do some trees, such as maples, have those beautiful reds? Trees, using energy from sunlight, convert carbon dioxide and water from the air into sugars; these are used by the tree for energy for growth; the more sunlight, the more sugar produced. Certain chemicals in the leaf, in the presence of sugar, may turn the leaf red or orange. Because the connection between the leaf and the rest of the tree is being shut down, the sugar stays in the leaf and so does the color.

So you're wanting the most colorful leaves and want to know what type of weather to request from the Weather Genie. The best conditions are cloudless (so there is a maximum of sunlight energy), warm during the day (so the sugar conversion process can gop more rapidly), cool at night (at night, when the sugar is supposed to go from the leaves to the trunk, the process goes more slowly). This whole process is also triggered by some daylight length—the tree "knows" when to start leaf turning.

As I said, things change every day in October, and different types of trees or even individual trees change color to different colors, different extents, and at different times. For example, in early October the Black Locusts in the meadow south of the road between Yosemite Lodge and Yosemite Village are turning yellow, and the elm tree nearby is still green, as are the oaks in the same area. By the middle of October, the locust has lost most of its leaves and the elm tree is turning yellow, in contrast to the dark green leaved oaks. Park visitors are going wild looking at and photographing the beautiful symmetrical elm all alone in the meadow, and are ignoring the oaks. By the end of the month, the locust has no leaves left, and the elm's leaves are mostly brown; but the oaks leaves are now turning a combination of yellow and brown.

Other trees produce spectacular colors too. The Chokecherries in the Museum Garden have subtle reddish colors in their leaves; the Pacific Dogwoods have leaf colors from pale orange to dark red; the Bigleaf Maples have bright yellow leaves which gleam in the sunlight; and the Dwarf Maples (especially abundant in the Bungalow area of the Ahwahnee Hotel) have all combinations from green to yellow to orange to pale red.

A delightful drive this month is along Valley roads from Yosemite Lodge to Sentinel Bridge. Not only can you see the bright yellows of willlows and maples on the Valley Walls, but you can also see the bright yellows of Bigleaf Maples and California Black Oaks all along the road.

There are other things to look at this month. The apples in the three orchards in the Valley are now ripe. The Park Service does not object to people picking the apples (although the bears do!), but it's hard to reach them. Sometimes there are apples on the ground, and if they aren't too beat up from their fall they will probably taste pretty good. The best time to go apple hunting is after it has been windy (the apples also fall off the twigs because the connection between them is not strong enough).

November

Most of the leaves are gone from the broadleaved trees now, but two things about the leaves are great. First, there are large areas of them, and if you walk on them you can hear them crunch, a sound very pleasing to me. Second, you don't have to rake them!

A few broadleaved trees still have leaves; these "evergreen" trees include California Live Oak and California Bay; both can be seen on the cliffs, where they form most of the greenery.

It is interesting to me that in November California Bay has many tiny white flower buds which seem about to open any day, but they won't actually open until March.

The conifers have many brown leaves now, but these will fall this month, and next spring green leaves will replace them.

This month it's the Incense Cedar's turn to shed pollen, and there will be a lot because there are so many Incense Cedars in the Valley.

December

Snow once again comes to the Valley Floor. Besides the things seen in January, you can also go to one of the areas with old California Black Oak trees (the Village near Bus Stops 6 and 9 is a good place, as is the Ahwahnee lawn) and look for Dwarf Mistletoe. This grows on the limbs of the oaks, and looks like a small bush with lots of leaves. If the sky is overcast, stand under a tree and point your camera straight up like I have done, and you can get pictures which look like Abstract Art.

This concludes Adventure 8; but by now you probably know enough to jump off and answer some of your own questions.

SUGGESTED READING

In Print, At Present for Sale in Valley Bookstores

Arno, S. F., 1973, "Discovering Sierra Trees", Yosemite Assoc., Yosemite, Cal., 88 pp.
    —Identification and description of most trees in this book

Berry, J. B., 1966, "Western Forest Trees", Dover Publications, New York, 238 pp.
    —Identification and description of most trees in this book, including their uses

DeMars, S. E., 1991, "The Tourist in Yosemite, 1855-1985", Univ. Utah Press, Salt Lake City, 168 pp.
    —Tells the history of tourism in the Valley

Hutchings, J. M., 1990, "In the Heart of the Sierras", Ed. by Peter Browning, Great West Books, Lafayette, Cal., 595 pp.
    —A travelogue of the Valley written in the 1880s

Little, E. L., 1980, "Audubon Society Field Guide of North American Trees—Western Region", Alfred A. Knopf, New York, 639 pp.
    —Identification and description of Valley trees, with great pictures

Peattie, D. C., 1950, "A Natural History of Western Trees", Houghton Mifflin Company, Boston, 751 pp.
    —Identification and description of Valley trees

Peterson, P. V. and P. V. Peterson Jr., "Native Trees of the Sierra Nevada", Cal. Nat. Hist. Guides n. 36, Univ. Cal. Press, Berkeley, Cal., 146 pp.
    —Identification and description of Valley trees

Russell, C. P., 1992, "One Hundred Years in Yosemite", Yosemite Assn., Yosemite, Cal., 269 pp.
—Documents the history of the Valley; has chronology

Storer, T. I. and R. L. Usinger, "Sierra Nevada Natural History", Univ. Cal. Press, Berkeley, Cal., 374 pp.
—Gives a review of Geology, Botany, Zoology in the Sierra; good illustrations and descriptions of our trees

Watts, Tom, 1973, "Pacific Coast Tree Finder", Nature Study Guild, Berkeley, Cal., 61 pp.
—Small, inexpensive book for identifying Sierra trees

Yosemite Association, no date, "The Indian People of Yosemite", leaflet, 8 pp.
—Pamphlet sold in Indian Village at back of Yosemite Museum

Shelved at Yosemite National Park Research Library

Acree, L. N., 1993, "Plant Communities of Yosemite Valley", National Park Service, Resources Management Division, Yosemite National Park, 23 pp.
—Present-day status of vegetation in the Valley

Brockman, C. F., 1948, "Broadleaved Trees of Yosemite National Park", Yosemite Nature Notes, v. XXVI, n. 1, pp. 1-40.
—Good reference for Yosemite trees but out of print

Cole, James E., (1939, Rev. 1963 by W. R. Jones), "Cone-Bearing Trees of Yosemite National Park", Yosemite Nat. Hist. Assn., Yosemite National Park, Cal., 52 pp.
—Good reference for Yosemite trees but out of print

Foley, D. J., 1901, "Yosemite Souvenir and Guide", Pub. by Author, 105 pp.
—Guidebook for Yosemite Park

Gibbens, R. P. and H. F. Heady, 1964, "The Influence of Modern Man on the Vegetation of Yosemite Valley", Univ. Cal. Div. Agricultural Sciences, 44 pp.
    —Details changes in Valley vegetation since 1851

Greene, L. W., 1987, "Yosemite: The Park and Its Resources", U, S, Dept. of Interior, National Park Service, 3 vols., 1251 pp.
    —Comprehensive history of Yosemite since 1851

Hall, A. F., 1929, "Yosemite Valley; An Intimate Guide", Natl. Parks Pub. House, Berkeley, Cal., 80 pp.
    —Guidebook for the Valley

Harlow, W. M., 1970, "Inside Wood—Masterpiece of Nature", American Forestry Assn., New York, 120 pp.
    —Explains about wood and has marvelous cross sections of trees

Heady, H. F. and P. J. Zinke, 1978, "Vegetational Changes in Yosemite Valley", Nat. Park Ser. Occasional Paper Five, 25 pp.
    —Similar to Gibbens and Heady

Jackson, H. H., 1971, "Ah-Wah-Ne Days—A Visit to the Yosemite Valley in 1872", The Book Club of San Francisco, San Francisco, Reprint, 84 pp.
    —Nostalgic look at Yosemite Valley

Leidig, Jack, 1941, "Other Early-Day Buildings", Notes in Yosemite Research Library, 11 pp.
    —Recollections of Yosemite Valley history circa 1900

Merriam, C. Hart., 1917, "Indian Village and Camp Sites in Yosemite Valley", Sierra Club Bull. 10, No. 2, p. 202-209; in Greene, L. W., 1987, "Yosemite: The Park and Its Resources", U. S. Dept. of Interior, 3 vols., 1251 pp.
    —Gives names and locations of Indian Villages in Yosemite Valley

Orland, Ted, "Man And Yosemite—A Photographer's View of the Early Years", The Image Continuum Press, Santa Cruz, Cal., 95 pp.
—Shows in photos how Valley vegetation has changed since 1851

Robinson, Homer W., 1948, "The History of Business Concessions in Yosemite National Park", Yosemite Nature Notes, V. XXVII, No. 6, pp. 84-90
—Summary article about businesses in the Valley

Sudworth, G. B., 1908, "Forest Trees of the Pacific Slope", U. S. Govt. Printing Off., Washington, D. C., 441 pp.
—Classic book describing trees from the Sierra and other areas

Tressider, Mary and Della Hoss, 1932, "The Trees of Yosemite", Stanford Univ. Press, Palo Alto, Cal., 133 pp.
—Good reference for Yosemite trees but out of print

APPENDIX A

Yosemite Valley Puzzle "Answers"

Although these are my answers to the questions posed in Adventure 2, they only seem the best answers at this time. Like you, I am still learning every day, and my answers might change next month. For today, here are my answers:

[2.2] (Why are there different species of dogwoods in the Eastern and Western United States?)

Between the eastern and western parts of the U. S. there is a large area with essentially no dogwoods because there is not enough precipitation for them to grow. As one goes into Mexico, the climate is too hot and too dry; as one goes into northern Canada, the climate is too cold in the winter for dogwoods to survive. Thus, the trees in the two parts of the country could evolve separately.

[2.3] (Is the Ponderosa Pine in front of the Village Store one or two trees?)

I favor two trees. From my observations, Ponderosas do split but usually much higher in the tree. It is easy for me to believe that two seeds could sprout at the same time and grow taller at just about the same rate and that the root systems could merge.

Of course, the best way to find out would be to cut down the tree and see whether there are one or two sets of rings at ground level, but I would rather be able to look at the tree!

[2.4] (Why are the Giant Sequoias in the Ahwahnee parking lot different sizes?)

There are all sorts of possible reasons for this; the one that comes to mind first is that the tallest trees are on the western edge of the east-west-trending set of trees. Giant Sequoias are very intolerant of shade, and the one on the west end (which is the tallest and widest) could have cut down sunlight for the others during the afternoon. Another possible explanation is that the soil might be better for growing these trees in some sites than others.

[2.5] (Why does ring thickness change around the stump and why are some rings thinner than others?)

When a conifer tree starts to lean (which many do), the tree commonly builds a greater thickness of wood on the side away from which the tree is leaning (this is called "compression reaction wood") in an effort to pull the tree back to vertical (incidentally, broadleaved trees commonly build more wood on the side toward which the tree is leaning).

One explanation for rings which don't go all the way around the tree is that the cambium was not protected by the bark on one side, and as a result was not making new cells. Three ways this could happen are if a forest fire burned the bark, a porcupine gnawed the bark, or a rock or a falling tree stripped the bark.

[2.7] (What caused the holes in the Ponderosa Pine logs at Lower Yosemite Falls?)

Although I have never actually seen this happen to these logs, it looks like a woodpecker looking for insects drilled holes into the trunk (insects dig into the sapwood of trees and the woodpeckers can apparently locate them by sound).

[2.8] (Why are White Firs so popular at Christmastime?)

This young tree has a symmetrical cone shape and the branches are dense but not too dense. As a result, you can see tinsel, ornaments and light bulb strings you hang on the tree. Also, the branches of five-to-eight-footers are strong enough to hold ornaments but flexible enough that they droop gracefully; and the needles keep the hooks on the ornaments from sliding off the branches.

Young Douglas Fir trees (seen best at Stops 12 and 16) are similar but the branches are not as strong; so they droop a little more than White Fir branches. Some people find this droop very graceful and the tree's natural aroma pleasing. For these reasons Douglas Firs are more popular Christmas trees.

[2.11] (Why are there plentiful Canyon Live Oaks yet scarce tall conifers on the Valley Walls?)

Where there are plentiful Canyon Live Oaks, there is usually a talus slope (essentially a pile of rocks fallen from weaknesses in the rock above); and this talus slope usually has a rich dark soil. The Canyon Live Oaks growing there provide dense shade, which prevents Ponderosas, for example, from growing.

[2.17] (How did the house-sized boulder get into the middle of Tenaya Creek?)

There are two likely explanations. The first explanation is that a huge volume of rock fell from the cliffs above when the stresses on it overcame the natural rock strength; when it hit the canyon bottom, it shattered into smaller fragments, catapulting the largest fragment (this boulder) into what is now Tenaya Creek.

The second explanation is that this rock fell from a cliff onto a glacier (a river of moving ice) which was present in this area during the Ice Age. The rock was transported on top of the ice downhill as on a conveyor belt. At some point, the ice melted and the rock slowly, gently settled into where it is now.

APPENDIX

Remnants of the Old Village

Below is a list of notes I made about buildings and remnants in the Old Village.

To make the accompanying map I used the following sources:

1. Three surveyed appraisal maps made in 1924
2. A 1956 Auto Map of the Old Village
3. A 1920 map from a Yosemite guidebook
4. 1:24,000 (2000 feet per inch) topographic maps of Yosemite Valley dated 1907, 1919, 1934, 1947, 1958, 1961, 1976, 1988.

The dates (when each building was erected and removed) are my best estimates based on a series of maps and other types of information; although some of these are probably inaccurate, this is the only compilation I have seen to the present time.

Buildings on 1924 maps

Building 1: Upper Hotel/Hutching's/Coulter & Murphy's/Cedar
   Cottage (1859/1941)
   Nail holes in Incense Cedar tree "Big Tree"
   Two bronze plaques commemorating corners of the Big Tree
      Room
   Three bronze plaques commemorating corners of the hotel

Building 2: Oak Cottage (1898/1941)
   Smooth rock slab (fireplace?)
   Two bronze plaques commemorating corners of the hotel
   Two places of exposed corrugated steel sewer pipe
   Two Bigleaf Maple trees

Building 3: Rock Cottage (1870/1937)
    Exposed terra cotta sewer pipe

Building 4: Dynamite Storage/Jail (1912/1959 moved to Pioneer
    History Center)
    No remnants

Building 5: Stable (Before 1924/Between 1934 and 1947)
    No remnants

Building 6: Firehouse (Before 1924/Between 1925 and 1934)
    No remnants

Building 7: Stegman's Seeds/Sinning's Woodworking Gallery/
    Sierra Club Reading Room/Fiske Sales Gallery (Before 1875/
    After 1913, before 1924)
    Three eye bolts in rock beside building site
    Two sides fit recess in rock

Building 8: YNP Residence (Before 1924/Before 1934)
    Low rock wall in front of building

Building 9: Wells Fargo/NPS Residence; part of this called "Hope
    Cottage" (1910/About 1959 moved to Pioneer History Center)
    Fallen Incense Cedar tree with insulator and wires
    Low rock wall in front of building

Building 10: Fiske Residence/NPS Residence (Before 1920/
    Between 1947 and 1958)
    No remnants, but building is shaped like rock recess

Building 11: U. S. Commisioner's Residence (Before 1924/
    Between 1947 and 1958)
    No remnants, but parts of building fit rock recess

Building 12: YNP Meat Market (1911/Between 1956 and 1958)
    Pieces of concrete slab
    Rock with two eye bolts and two bolts
    Two pieces of steel pipe
    Several Bigleaf Maples in a group
    Two sides fit rock recess

Building 13: Degnan Store (ca. 1900/1959)
    Tree in front of store has wires about 20 feet up

Building 14: Degnan Second Residence (ca. 1900/1981)
    (Bakery corner of residence moved to Pioneer History Center
    in Wawona)
    Chunks of concrete
    Bigleaf Maple in yard
    High rock with spike on top

Building 15: Degnan Storage (ca. 1900/1980?)
    Concrete footings
    Large rock toward Chapel with spike on top

Building 16: Degnan Barn (ca. 1900/1980?)
    Piece of sewer pipe exposed

Building 17: Degnan First Residence (1870s/Before 1924)
    All sorts of concrete, pipe, etc.
    Concrete footings attached to rocks
    Four Bigleaf Maples seem to have been landscaped in front
        yard

Building 18: Johnny Finch's Blacksmith Shop (No dates, but on
    Auto Guide Map as a building standing before 1925)
    Flat spot near, but not on, Auto Map site just the right size for
        the building
    Two rocks with iron rings
    Rock with spike on top

Building 19: Degnan Chicken House/Stable (ca. 1890/after 1924)
    No remnants, but three sides fit recess in rocks

Building 20: YNP Storage and Residence ("Wiggle Inn") (ca.
    1912/Between 1946 and 1958)
    No remnants

Building 21: Salter's Warehouse and Stables/YNP Storage and
    Residence/Masonic Temple (1900 or after/Between 1976
    and 1988)
    No remnants, but three sides fit recess in rocks

Building 22: Yosemite Valley Chapel (1879 — moved to Village from near Four-Mile Trail in 1902/ Still standing)

Building 23: Pillsbury Darkroom (1907?/1926?)
   No remnants

Building 24: Pillsbury Darkroom and Garage (1907?/1926?)
   No remnants

Building 25: Hallett-Taylor/Studio of the Three Arrows/Pillsbury's Pictures (1900?/1926?)
   No remnants

Building 26: Sinning's Wood Shop/Starke's/Dexter's/NPS Residence (After 1900/Before 1934)
   No remnants

Building 27: Post Office (1920/1959)
   No remnants

Building 28: Garibaldi's "New" Store/Salter's/Thornton's/YNP General Store (ca. 1900 moved from across street/1959)
   No remnants

Building 29: Reilly Studio/Fagersteen Studio/Boysen Studio (1875/ 1926)
   Incense Cedar tree next to bike path fits into recess of building
   Apple tree

Building 30: Boysen Studio (1900 or after/1926)
   Sugar maple tree originally in east yard
   Sidewalk in front

Building 31: Boysen Darkroom (1900 or after/1926)
   No remnants

Building 32: Foley Studio/Yosemite Falls Studio (1891/1926)
   Sidewalk in front

Building 33: ?Fiske's Studio/Army Administration Building/
    NPS Adminstration Building (Before 1904?/1925)
    Sidewalk in front, which widens in front of building
    Raised curb on street side of sidewalk

Building 34: NPS Woodshed (Before 1924/Before 1934)
    No remnants

Building 35: Best's Studio (1902/1926)
    Sidewalk in front of building
    Elm stumps between sidewalk and street
    Rock with iron ring and Indian mortar hole
    Apple tree

Building 36: YNP Residence (Before 1924/Between 1956 and
    1958)
    No remnants

Building 37: NPS Pavilion (1901/1963)
    Six-inch-wide strip of asphalt next to concrete sidewalk
        (probably a walkway)

Building 38: Cosmopolitan Saloon/Guardian's Office/Locust
    Cottage/YNP General Offices (1871/1932)
    Sidewalk in front of building — angle changes in front of
        building
    Plum tree in yard
    Elm sprouts in stump shapes between sidewalk and road

Building 39: YNP Toilet (Before 1924/ Between 1934 and 1947)
    No remnants

Building 40: YNP Offices (Before 1924/Between 1934 and 1947)
    No remnants

Building 41: YNP Engineer Offices (Before 1924/1941?)
    No remnants

Building 42: Yosemite Stage and Transportation Office/YNP
    General Offices (Before 1924/1941?)
    No remnants

Building 43: Ivy Cottage, also called "New Saloon" (1900/1938)
Sidewalk in front of building

Building 44: YNP Residence (Before 1924/1938?)
No remnants

Building 45: River Cottage (1870/1938)
Sidewalk in front of building
Bronze commemorative marker on rock

Building 46: Yosemite Falls Hotel/Yosemite Park Hotel/Sentinel
Hotel (1876/1938)
Sidewalk in front of building
Remains of rock wall at edge of river
Rectangular manhole in sidewalk
Square re-concreted areas in sidewalk where pillars were
Notch in pine-cedar forest on north side of Valley where trees
were cut down for view

Building 47: Old Bathhouse (1886/Before 1924)
No remnants

Building 48: Bluebird Cottage, used as YNP Employee Housing
(ca. 1900/1941?)
No remnants

Building 49: YNP Employee Laundry (ca. 1900/Between 1976
and 1988)
Wires on tree in rocks near building

Building 50: Fox Cottage, used as YNP Employee Housing (ca.
1900/Between 1924 and 1934)
No remnants

Building 51: YNP Ice House (1900/Between 1961 and 1976)
Rock wall on side of building

Building 52: YNP Print Shop (ca. 1900/Between 1924 and 1934)
No remnants

Building 53: Oriental Cottage, used as YNP Employee Housing
(ca. 1900/Between 1924 and 1934)
No remnants

Buildings not on 1924 maps

Building 54: Blacksmith Shop (Before 1924/Before 1924)
No remnants

Building 55: State of California Carpenter Shop (1870s?/Before
1924)
Electrical conduit cemented into rock next to possible site
Spike on top of rock

Building 56: State of California Barn (?Late 1870s/Between 1911
and 1924)
Pieces of concrete slab on end away from road

Building 57: J. J. Westfall Meat Market (1892/1905-06); shown
on site of Degnan Second Residence, but then structures
would overlap; possibly near here
No remnants

Building 58: J. J. Westfall stables (1892/1905-06); shown on site
of Degnan Second Residence, but then structures would overlap;
possibly near here
No remnants

Building 59: Cavagnaro Store/Garibaldi's Store (1881/1900);
shown on Auto Guide Map as fronting between two trees,
which may be the oak tree and oak snag near the Chapel; more
or less on the site of Pillsbury's Pictures, Building 25; moved
across street to later location of General Store, Building 28
No remnants

Other remnants not next to buildings

Giant Sequoia tree between Sentinel Hotel and Oak Cottage

Two Giant Sequoia trees between River Cottage and Oak Cottage

Iron ring on rock between River Cottage and Oak Cottage

Wire on fallen oak tree near the two Giant Sequoias

Spike on top of rock near stump of fallen oak tree

"Native Son Sequoia" tree between Sinning's and Cosmopolitan

Mortar holes in flat rock alongside flat path leading south from Bluebird Cottage

Sawed-off telephone poles next to this rock

Sawed-off telephone pole in flat area southeast of Rock Cottage

Pottery and bottle fragments

Iron ring on rock near path between Johnny Finch's and Wiggle Inn

APPENDIX C

Common and Latin Names

Different people refer to the same tree with different common names. For example, Canyon Live Oak is also called "Maul Oak"; and Douglas Fir has at least 21 different common names! Here is a listing of common names used in this book and their Latin equivalents:

Common Name	Latin Name
American Elm	*Ulmus americana*
Apple	*Malus spp.*
Bigleaf Maple	*Acer macrophyllum*
Birchleaf Mountain Mahogany	*Cercocarpus betuloides*
Black Cottonwood	*Populus microcarpa*
Black Locust	*Robinia pseudoacacia*
Blue Elderberry	*Sambucus caerulea* (or *glauca*)
Bush Lupine	*Lupinus albifrons*
California Bay (or Laurel)	*Umbellularia californica*
California Black Oak	*Quercus kelloggii*
California Blackberry	*Rubus ursinus* (or *vitifolius*)
California Buckeye	*Aesculus californica*
California Hazelnut	*Corylus rostrata*
California Redbud	*Cercis occidentalis*
California Wild Grape	*Vitis californica*
California Wild Rose	*Rosa spp.*
Canyon Live Oak	*Quercus chrysolepsis*
Chokecherry	*Prunus demissa*
Coast Redwood	*Sequoia sempervirens*
Corn Lily	*Veratrum californicum*
Creamberry	*Holodiscus discolor*
Creek Dogwood	*Cornus californica* (or *stolonifera*)

<u>Common Name</u>   <u>Latin Name</u>

Common Name	Latin Name
Deer Brush	*Ceanothus integerrimus*
Douglas Fir	*Pseudotsuga menziesii*
Evening Primrose	*Oenothera hookeri*
Giant Sequoia	*Sequoiadendron giganteum*
Gray Pine	*Pinus sabiniana*
Incense Cedar	*Calocedrus decurrens*
Jeffrey Pine	*Pinus jeffreyi*
Knobcone Pine	*Pinus attenuata* (or *tuberculata*)
Lodgepole Pine	*Pinus murryana* (or *contorta*)
Manzanita	*Arctostaphylos spp.*
Mock Orange	*Philadelphus lewisii*
Mountain Ash	*Sorbus sitchensis*
Mountain Hemlock	*Tsuga mertensiana*
Mountain Spirea	*Spiraea densiflora*
Pacific Dogwood	*Cornus nuttallii*
Ponderosa Pine	*Pinus ponderosa*
Quaking Aspen	*Populus tremuloides*
Red Fir	*Abies magnifica*
Rocky Mountain Maple	*Acer glabrum*
Scouler Willow	*Salix nuttallii*
Sierra Coffeeberry	*Rhamnus rubra*
Sierra Juniper	*Juniperis occidentalis*
Silk Tassel	*Garrya fremontii*
Snowberry	*Symphoricarpos albus*
Spice Bush	*Calycanthus occidentalis*
Sugar Pine	*Pinus lambertiana*
Tanbark Oak	*Lithocarpus densiflora*
Thimbleberry	*Rubus parviflorus*
Western Azalea	*Rhododendron occidentale*
White Alder	*Alnus rhombifolia*
White Fir	*Abies concolor*
Willow	*Salix spp.*

GLOSSARY

Barb: A very short leaf, sharp at the end pointed away from the trunk; the leaf shape of Giant Sequoia.

Branch scars: Irregularities in bark formed when branches fall off or are cut off.

Bric-a-brac: Decorative wooden articles usually sold in gift shops.

Broadleaved tree: Trees with flattish leaves; technically, Angiosperms.

Browse: The part of the tree which animals eat.

Cambium layer: The layer of wood in a tree where cells are actively dividing; the tree cannot grow when this layer is absent or destroyed.

Compound leaf: A leaf composed of several individual leaflets occurring together in certain plants.

Cone: A woody, commonly round structure in some trees which contains and protects the tree's seeds.

Conifer: Commonly, "evergreen" trees which produce cones; technically, Gymnosperms.

Duff: Partly decayed plant matter on forest floor.

Evergreen: A plant whose leaves are green all year.

Firefall: A tourist attraction of Yosemite Valley in which burning bark was dumped off Glacier Point nightly to create the effect of a burning waterfall; this practice was discontinued in 1968.

Fleur-de-lis: Literally, "the flower of the lily"; stylized to make the emblem of France; the shape of iris flowers, and an apt description of Incense Cedar cones.

Foliage: The leaves or needles of a plant.

Fungus: a plant which receives part or all of its energy from other plants rather than sunlight.

Glaciation: The geologic process by which ice shapes mountains and valleys.

Gnarled: Describes a shape which is twisted, rugged or irregular in some other way.

Granary: In Yosemite Valley, a container Indians used to store acorns.

Hazard trees: Trees in Yosemite deemed by the National Park Service as a hazard to humans and consequently to be cut down.

Heartwood: The part of the tree trunk filled with resin; this gives the tree strength to keep standing.

High Country: The name colloquially given to the area of Yosemite National Park above Yosemite Valley.

Leaflet: A single leaf in a tree with compound leaves.

Medial moraine: A hill formed by rocks and soil scraped off mountainsides where two glaciers met; remain after glacier has melted.

Mono Winds: Winds generated during storms which howl through Yosemite Valley; strong enough to break Valley trees.

Needle: An individual leaf of a conifer tree, so named because of its long, narrow shape.

Paper pulp: The soft wood of certain trees which is used in the manufacture of paper.

Resin: A substance manufactured by the tree which may either contain fluids necessary for tree growth (in the sapwood) or harden to strengthen the tree (in the heartwood).

Rose hips: The part of the rose flower developed to contain seeds; sometimes used as a cosmetic.

Rounds: Cylinders of tree trunk cut about two feet thick and often used for seats in Yosemite Valley.

Sapling: A young tree.

Sapwood: The part of the tree through which are conducted fluids essential to the tree's life and growth.

Shade tolerance: The amount of low-light level a particular species of tree can tolerate and still thrive.

Shrub: Like a tree, but (usually) at maturity less than 12 feet high, with several trunks, each of which is less than three inches in diameter: in certain conditions, a tree of a certain species may be considered a shrub.

Talus slope: A steep-angled rock pile caused when the Valley wall is attacked by frost action; frequently has few trees or shrubs.

Tap root: A vertical root sent down from the middle of the trunk in some kinds of trees to ensure a more steady supply of water.

Tree rings: Concentric or nearly concentric structures seen when the tree trunk is cut perpendicularly to its long dimension.

Unfavorable location: A place where a particular tree starts to grow with soil or light conditions unfavorable for best growth.

Valley Rim: In Yosemite Valley, the tops of the cliffs.

Watercourse: The course of a river or stream, along which certain kinds of trees grow.

Wood rays: Structures in some kinds of trees which cross tree rings and provide the tree with communication between different parts of the tree.

Woodenware: Dishes, bowls, etc. made of wood from certain trees.

INDEX

Wide- (eye)d Publications

P. O. Box 964   Carnelian Bay, CA 96140

(916) 546-1149   FAX (916) 546-5948

Did you borrow this book from a friend and want one of your very own?

Looking for a great gift for someone?

WE HAVE THE ANSWERS TO THESE QUESTIONS!

(Just fill in the blanks below)

Please send me ___ copies of:

"TREE ADVENTURES IN YOSEMITE VALLEY"

NAME _____
ADDRESS _____
_____
_____

(Plesase enclose a check or money order for $7.95; California residents add $0.62 state sales tax)

Watch for "TREE ADVENTURES IN TAHOE" around Christmas...